Christian Outlines

Christian Outlines

An Introduction to Religion

By

Cyril Alington

Head Master of Eton, Chaplain to H.M. the King
Hon. Fellow of Trinity College, Oxford

London

Ivor Nicholson & Watson Ltd
44 Essex Street, Strand, W.C.2

1932

First published in 1932

Made and Printed in Great Britain by Butler & Tanner Ltd., Frome and London

Preface

THIS little book, as its title implies, attempts no more than an outline. It is an outline which needs filling up at every stage, but those who have to "teach religion" will agree that it is at least as important that the right questions should be asked as that the answers given should be completely satisfactory, and I have tried to suggest lines of thought which will provoke the right sort of question. I have refrained from exhortation, because that belongs rather to the spoken than to the written word, and no one can be more conscious than the writer that any value it may have will depend upon the good will of those who use it, and on their readiness to put life into its dry bones.

Contents

Prologue

CHRISTIANITY offers an explanation of the world in which we live. It is impossible, or should be impossible, not to seek for such an explanation, and though no explanation that we can give is likely to be complete, we must seek for one which takes account of the most important facts: if we are right, as we surely are, in thinking that nothing has been created greater than man, our explanation must account for him and for his hopes. Christianity desires to provide such an explanation, and it is from this point of view that we have first to consider it. If this leads us, as it must, into large and difficult questions, we must remember that to explain the universe cannot in the nature of things be a simple task: to refuse to think is to give up before we have begun: and it is only people who refuse to think who suppose the Christian answer to be more difficult than any other.

Any modern scientific treatise would show them their mistake: the simple fact is that the

universe *is* a "Mysterious Universe" and that
any attempt to explain it leads us into regions
which baffle our powers of thought and im-
agination. The explanation which Christianity gives is not an intellectual certainty: if it
were there would be no spiritual value in accepting it: but it is a theory which does explain the
world, for it explains it as having a purpose,
and that is the only explanation of anything
with which the mind of man is satisfied.[1]

From another point of view Christianity is
a historical institution. It has its roots in
certain facts of history which can be examined
like other historical facts. We can see how
it began, how it grew and how it is still growing,
and can learn both from its successes and
from its failures. It brings new ideas into
the world, and it is the truth and falsehood of
those ideas which matter more than the way
in which they have been hitherto translated
into action, for a principle does not become

[1] St. Augustine summed up the Christian theory when he
wrote "Thou hast made us for Thyself, O Lord, and our
heart is restless until it finds rest in Thee," and what he
wrote of the heart of man is equally true of his brain: it is
significant that a great man of science like Sir James Jeans
sums up the present conclusion of his investigations by
saying: "We discover that the universe shows evidence of
a designing or controlling power that has something in
common with our own individual minds" (*The Mysterious
Universe*, p. 149).

better or worse according to the way in which people act up to it.

Lastly, we have to think of Christianity as a guide to our own lives, the following of a divine pattern, the loyalty to a divine Master. No single sentence of a Christian Father contains more practical theology than the words "Christ became human that we might become divine," for in it we read both of the purpose of God for man and of the way in which it has been, and is being, fulfilled. Man, as we believe, was made in the image of God, and it is through Christ's earthly life that we are shown the road which we must travel to make real the divine part of us and so to come in the end to the perfect vision of God which is the goal of all human endeavour.

These are the three aspects of Christianity of which we are to attempt to present an outline.

I

Belief in God

IF you look in a learned book for a definition
of Religion you will be told that it means
our dealings with "powers superior to man
which are believed to direct and control the
course of nature and of human life," and that
will do to begin with, though there are two
or three points in the definition which want
explaining.

In the first place when we say "powers"
we must mean "personal beings": if you
believe, as some people do, that the world
is governed by Forces or Laws which are
not personal you cannot have any religion,
though you may try to work on them by
magical rites and ceremonies. It is very
hard to explain what we mean by "persons,"
but if you think of the differences between
a plant and a fish and a dog and a man you
will see that you are going up in the scale,
and that a man, who can remember and hope
and make long plans and think about other
people and other things, is much more "per-

sonal" than any of the others. Religious
people believe that the Power which made
us so "personal" must be "personal" itself:
otherwise we cannot understand how we came
to exist, for man cannot be created by anything
inferior to himself, and a power which was not
personal would be inferior, just as the best
motor-car is a thing inferior to the man who
made it. So the first thing we have to say
about our definition is that Religion is concerned not with blind Forces and unchanging
Laws but with a Person or Persons superior
to man who are believed to direct and control
our lives.[1]

Then you will notice the words "are believed
to direct," and I hope you will not be frightened by them. People often talk as if Religion
was inferior to other kinds of learning because
they deal with things which we *know*, while
it only deals with things which we *believe*:
but, as a matter of fact, there are very few
things indeed which we really know. Some
people would say that the only things we really
know are simple mathematical facts such as
"twice two are four," and that we only know
that because we settled beforehand that that
was what the answer was going to be: but
even if you do not go as far as that and look
at Science (which ought to mean knowing)

[1] See Note A at end of chapter.

you will find that the best men of science
do not claim to *know* very much. They dis-
believe a great deal which other men of science
believed fifty years ago, and they are always
questioning their own conclusions.[1] They *believe* they have found out a great deal and
are always hoping to find out more, and in
that they are just like men of religion. They
have one great advantage, because it is easier
to test their results, but it is quite wrong to
think that their way of learning is different
from that of other people: all knowledge starts
by believing, by men making the best guess
they can, and testing it in every possible way,
and that is what religious people do, or ought
to do. After all, the things of which we feel
most certain, such as the love of our parents
or the trustworthiness of our friends, are
things which do not admit of demonstration,
so that there is no reason to regard the absence
of mathematical certainty as in any way fatal.

No doubt it would be very convenient if we
could absolutely prove the existence of these
"personal agents" we spoke about, but if you
will think a little you will see that absolute
proof is almost impossible and will not worry
about it. There is a monument in Devizes

[1] The man of science, says Professor Jeans, is accustomed
to the reproach that he changes his views all the time (*The
Mysterious Universe*, p. 147).

market-place to a woman who died directly she had said "May God strike me dead if I am telling a lie," but that sort of argument does not impress many people, and the more you think, the harder you will find it to discover any argument which would certainly convince everyone that God exists. There is a great text in the Epistle to the Hebrews which says "He that cometh to God must believe that He is and that He is a rewarder of them that diligently seek Him," and that is where we must begin. We must assume that God exists, because we shall never get any absolute proof of it, and we must assume that He wants us to know Him, for of course if He wanted to remain unknown we should never get very far. Those are the two assumptions which every religious person has to make, and we make them in just the same way, and in just the same spirit, as that in which men of science make the assumptions, such as that of the uniformity of nature or the conservation of energy, which have at various times helped them to get on with their work.

Now let us go back to our definition. You will see that it uses the plural, "powers", and there are some religions which worship many gods of different degrees of power. The Hindus do so now, as the Greeks did, and when you read Greek literature you will find a great many stories of how these gods interfered with one another and had very undignified quarrels. But the Greeks, who were very clever people, came to see that this was not a good explanation of the world, and more and more they tended to put the supreme power in the hands of one deity and to pass, as we say, from polytheism to monotheism and the worship of one God. This came simply as a result of hard thinking, and almost all great thinkers and philosophers agree that behind the world there must be one Supreme Power whether they think of that Power as personal or not.

Besides polytheism, or the worship of many gods, there is another theory which divides the power between a Good God and an Evil God, just as time is divided between Light and Darkness: that is probably how the idea started and it is a simple way of explaining why things go wrong in the world, but it has never commended itself to thinkers, who feel certain that the world is one and must be created and controlled by one power only.

If that is so it would seem that we have to choose between a blind Force (something merely impersonal), a bad God (the devil), or a good God as the Supreme Power behind the world. We have already spoken of the first of these possibilities, and we need not spend very long in discussing the second. No doubt it is *conceivable* that the world was made by a bad and cruel god and that to do wrong is the way to win his favour. If that were so, a "religious" man would have to make up his mind whether it was better to serve this God or to obey those instincts which we call conscience which tell him the difference between right and wrong. He would find himself asking where these instincts come from, and would probably decide that as they seem part of his very being he must be wrong in his belief that he was made by an evil god.

For really these ideas go a very long way to prove the belief which lies at the back of practically all religion, that the world is really the work of a good God. However little men may be inclined to be brave or kind or honest or unselfish we find that all of them admire these qualities in other people, and have some dim desire to possess them. We hear a great deal of the Mystery of Evil, but it is really far more mysterious that all of us should admire qualities which we do not possess, when it would be so much more convenient to deny their goodness. No doubt we sometimes do this, but the most remarkable thing about everyone who can be called a man is that he has a standard of goodness to which, when he is at his best, he is trying to attain. His ideas of goodness will differ greatly in different times and countries, but the desire is always there, and apart from revelation (or a direct message from God to man) it is the strongest evidence for the goodness of the God who made us.[1]

There are some people who will think that an equally strong argument can be made from the beauty of the world, and our power of appreciating it,[2] or from the desire for Truth which exists in all men, and these are things which should never be forgotten; but the first argument is really strong enough to bear all the weight, and is the one to which "religious" people most naturally appeal. A religious man, then, is pre-eminently one who makes the assumption that behind the world there is a good God, who desires that His creatures should know Him; and religion begins with the effort to find out as much as possible of the nature of this God and the life which He desires man to lead. This is, or may be, a matter only of theory, but true religion cannot stop there. The more it knows of God, the more it must desire to worship Him in the ways which He would desire, and the more it learns of His purposes for mankind, the more it must desire to fulfil them, so that

---

[1] See Note B at end of chapter.
[2] See Note C at end of chapter.

the religious man is one who tries to worship
God as well as he can, and to live his life
(and to help others to live theirs) in accordance
with God's purpose.

NOTE A

The difficulty about speaking of God as "personal" is
that we are always inclined to think of personality in *merely*
human terms, so that we form a picture of God in human
shape. This may be the only way in which we can think,
but it does not follow that it is true. When we say that
God is personal we mean that He has at least all the qualities
which are involved in a human personality, and very much
more besides. Just as an infant, though a "person," could
form no just conception of the personality of a man, so we
inevitably fail to conceive adequately of the personality of
God. Again, because we only see personality in human
forms it is not at all safe to assume that a human form is a
necessary condition for possessing it. We are made "in the
image of God" not in respect of our bodies but in respect
of the powers of our minds and spirits: to make God in our
bodily image is a very dangerous heresy. A "person" holds
together in a unity all the people he knows and all the things
he knows: he is the central pivot round which they (so to
speak) revolve: they are *his* friends, *his* relations, *his* experi-
ences: in the same way we believe that God, the Source of
all things, is the Person round Whom they revolve and on
Whom they depend.

NOTE B

It is commonly said that men differ so much in their moral
standards that we cannot come to any definite conclusion
about them. No doubt it is perfectly true that actions

which some primitive peoples think virtuous seem to us wicked and that different virtues are very differently looked upon at different times. But it has yet to be shown that any type of man has ever applauded cruelty *as such* or cowardice *as such* or impurity *as such*. When they seem to admire them it is really for some reason which we forget. Similarly, men's tastes seem to change because we forget what they really admire. You can admire furniture, for instance, for its workmanship, its material, or its design, and your conclusions will depend on which you think most important. A child's liking for bright colours is not a wrong thing but a right and natural one, though it may learn as it grows older that other considerations matter more. In the same way the cruelties which a savage may admire are not admired because they are cruel but because they imply a readiness to sacrifice oneself for the tribe or for the chief who represents it. Does anyone ever admire anything for an entirely bad reason? I think not.

NOTE C

The argument runs somewhat as follows: we perceive beauty through our eyes and ears which are parts of the body. These latter clearly have "a survival value," but this is not true of our æsthetic emotions, for the power of appreciating beauty cannot help the individual or the race to survive. Either, then, this power is a pure accident, which is very unlikely, or it is the gift of a Power which can itself appreciate such things, and must be what we call personal. In enjoying the beauty of a sunset the religious man believes himself to be thinking God's thoughts after Him: if he sees that "it is good," he believes that God has also seen its goodness.

II

God's Revelation of Himself

WE have said that all religions assume that God is willing to be known, and this involves that showing of Himself to man which we call "revelation." The existence of a conscience or a desire for truth in man, like the existence of order and of beauty in nature,[1] is a "revelation" of the character of the God who made the world: but almost all religions claim to be based on a revelation of a more direct kind. God has spoken to, or through, some man who is, as we say, "inspired" to hand the message on to others. There is a very real sense in which all great and good men are "inspired," but we usually keep the word for this special purpose.

These inspired messengers (who are called "prophets" not because they foretell the future, but because they tell out the truth) vary greatly

[1] Beauty does not really exist in nature, but in the mind of the person who sees it: the word could have no meaning in the planet Mars if there are no persons to appreciate it, and never have been.

in the amount and value of their message, but they have this in common—that they help men better to understand the nature of God. Sometimes they themselves write down the message they have received and sometimes it is written down by others: you will find examples of both types among the Jews, of whom Amos was probably the first to write down his own message. It is interesting from this point of view to compare the method of Christ with that of Mahomet. Mahomet wrote down all the revelations he received, and the Koran is the result, so that his followers keep exactly to his precepts. Christ (who was, from this point of view, the last of the Hebrew prophets) never, so far as we know, wrote anything (except when he wrote with his finger in the dust): his followers wrote down what they could remember of his teaching as best they could. We shall consider later on how different the results of these two methods have been.

For Christians, of course, the life and words of Christ are the supreme revelation of the nature and purposes of God, but this does not mean either that there is no more to be learnt or that no sound teaching has come from any other source. On the first point all that need now be said is that Our Lord himself spoke of the Holy Spirit which was to guide his followers "into all the truth": there were many things which he had to say to his disciples, but they "could not bear them now," so that it is quite wrong to speak or think as if there were no more to be learnt outside the covers of the New Testament. What we do believe is that no new truth that may be discovered will prove inconsistent with what Christ told us. If a homely simile may be used, we are like children putting together the pieces of a puzzle—we know in general terms what the picture is to be, and the most important pieces have been put once for all in their right place: but the picture is a large one, and there are many pieces for which the right place still needs to be found.

In this task—and this is the second point— we shall by no means despise any help we can get from the prophets of other religions. The days are gone when it was thought that all other faiths than Christianity were necessarily evil: it was never a Christian belief in the best sense of the word, for St. Paul spoke of other nations than the Jews who were "feeling after God," and their efforts have not been in vain. As he said on another occasion, God has "not left Himself without witness" among the heathen, and the truths which their great men have reached are part of God's own truth. Nowadays missionaries are not content to think or speak of the heathen as if they were altogether in the darkness of ignorance: they are always on the look out for the good points in other religions which need not be, and are not, altogether false because they are imperfect. Christians have much that they can learn from honest followers of Buddha or Mahomet, though we believe that we have much more which we can teach them.

And here perhaps is the right place to deal with two mistakes which are very often made. In the first place, no Christian should believe that the honest followers of an imperfect creed are going to be punished hereafter for the imperfection of their belief. They are like the people in Christ's parable "who knew not their Lord's will," who are in a far better position than those who knew it and refused to obey. If they have a real chance of learning and refuse to take it, their punishment is deserved; but if, through our carelessness, they have no chance of learning, or if we present the lesson badly and unattractively, it is clear that we, and not they, are responsible for their remaining in ignorance. It is a very gloomy thought that if the Christians whom Mahomet met in his early days had been better representatives of their faith, he might very probably have become an ardent Christian, and incalculable miseries might have been spared the world.

But there is also a second mistake which is more serious still, and that is the mistake of supposing that it does not matter what a man believes, provided he believes it honestly. You only have to think for a moment to see what nonsense this is and how absurd it would sound in any other connection. A man may honestly believe that he knows how to drive or to mend a motor-car, but that will not save him from a bad disaster if he is really ignorant, and in politics or in ordinary life immeasurable harm is done by honest people who have never really thought things out. It is quite true that they are morally much better than dishonest men, but they often do quite as much mischief. Once more a simple illustration will make the point clear. A cricket match is won by the side which makes the most runs, and it does not matter to the result whether they are made in good style or bad; again, a "bad" cricketer may often make more runs than a "good" one, but everyone who plays cricket knows that there are certain rules of play which make a man play better, and no one could be so foolish as wilfully to ignore them. A player with a good eye and a good wrist will do better than a well-trained player without them, even if he has been badly

25

taught; but it is clear that good teaching would have made him better still. In the same way it is perfectly true that many good Mahommedans or good Buddhists are better than many Christians: what we say is not that all Christians are superior to those who hold other religions, but that they have the true theory, and that the good Buddhist or the good Mahommedan would be better still if his theory of life were wholly good instead of being partly good and partly false. Any false belief which a man holds must do harm both to himself and to other people; the more firmly and honestly he holds it the greater the harm will be, and the harm which is done by false beliefs about religion is in proportion to the importance of the subject.

It is time to come back to the question of revelation in a wider sense. The good God in whom all theists believe must be the source of all that is good in the world and of all our powers of appreciating it. The good things in the world are generally divided into the (morally) Good, the Beautiful and the True; and different people and different races have (always, as we believe, under God's guidance or inspiration) made great discoveries in all these directions, and are making them still. It is clear, to give one example, that the Greeks had a great deal to teach the world about

Beauty and the laws of proportion, which can never be set aside; but that is not to say that a very different people, like the Chinese, have not other things to teach about the same subject.

Again, every great thinker, whether in ancient Greece or modern Germany, makes additions to our knowledge of Truth; and the man who is seeking after Truth is seeking to read the mysteries of God, whether he thinks of it in that way or not. It is very reasonable to believe that moral Goodness is the most important of the three, but that is no reason for forgetting that all three are divine, and that every discovery which is made in any of the three helps us to understand better the nature of God who made us all. Religion has often suffered from being confined entirely to moral questions, and it would be good for moralists, artists and philosophers or scientists to realize that their object is ultimately the same. For a Christian all knowledge is a road to God, or, to put it more accurately, a treading of one of the paths which God has made for those who wish to find Him. Some of the roads may be shorter and easier, some may offer better prospects than others, but they all lead to God, for "in Him are all the treasures of wisdom and knowledge hidden." And as for the individual worker, whatever his sphere of action may be, we have no doubt that he is guided by God's spirit—whether his work be in art or science or theology, we say with St. Paul, "all these things worketh that one and the selfsame spirit, dividing to every man severally as He will."

Our first chapter showed us the reasons for believing in a good God who directs and controls the course of nature and human life. We have now been considering some of the ways in which this good God reveals Himself. It is time to pass to the special ways which led up to that Christian revelation which we regard as the supreme showing forth of God to man.

III

The Revelation to the Jews

THE most remarkable instance of religious revelation to a particular nation is undoubtedly to be found in the Jews. There have always been people who have found it a difficulty that the Jews should be "the chosen people"—and no doubt there are many faults that can be found with them as a nation—but the difficulty really rests on a misunderstanding. The Jews were "chosen" to do a particular piece of work for the world, just as other races have been, and are, chosen for other purposes: it is no more surprising that they should be pre-eminent in their knowledge of religion and their devotion to it than that the Greeks should lead the world in matters of art, or the Romans in the study of law, or the Anglo-Saxon races in the matter of government. Races, like individual men, have their special gifts and their special work to do.

The difficulty really comes from mistaking the meaning of the word "chosen," which means not chosen for reward, but chosen for

a very difficult and honourable service. It is
a mistake which the Jews themselves were
very ready to make, and it is not mere fancy
to think that they are rightly called "sons of
Jacob," for he made just the same mistake
when he defrauded Esau of his birthright. It
was only by long and painful experience that
he learnt that to have the birthright meant the
obligation to a very difficult service, for which
he had to be laboriously trained. In the same
spirit the Jews, who were entrusted with a
special knowledge of God for the use of the
world, tried their best to keep it to themselves,
and regarded other races as their inferiors.
They failed in their mission, and the book of
Jonah, one of the latest in the Old Testament,
is a parable of their failure. But they did
not understand the parable, or at any rate did
not profit by it, and when they rejected Christ
they showed how little they understood why
they had been chosen. He came "to be a
light to lighten the Gentiles, and to be the
glory of his people Israel," but because of
their blindness what should have been their
glory has become their shame.

If we once understand what it means to be
a chosen people we shall be able to see that
the Jews had, and have, the qualities which
are most important for those entrusted with a
very precious gift. There is nothing more

remarkable in the history of nations than the faithfulness of the Jews to their beliefs and customs. As has just been said, they failed at the great moment in their history, and so the belief to which they cling is imperfect, but no one can help admiring the strength and pertinacity which they show. When you remember that they have had no country for hundreds of years, and have been persecuted with a severity hardly equalled in the case of any other nation, you will be amazed at their still existing as a people at all. Their whole history is a proof that they are not "God's favourites," for no people has suffered more, but that they do possess in a very remarkable degree that quality which makes them the best possible guardians of any valuable truth, and their record shows that their one desire was to learn the truth about God—the most important of all possible truths.

The Old Testament, as has often been said, is not a book, but a library—the library of a nation—and the remarkable thing is that this nation's library is entirely devoted to the dealings of God with man. It is so unlike any other collection of books that it is very hard for us to read it in the right way, and we shall only do so if we remember, to begin with, that it represents the thoughts of many different periods during which men were slowly growing in the knowledge of God. At first they knew Him very imperfectly, and ascribe to Him thoughts and words and deeds which we know to be quite out of keeping with His character. There can be no greater mistake than to suppose that a Christian is bound to accept the view of God which the Jews held in their earliest days, and no one would do so were it not that we often read the Old Testament without any historical sense, as if it were all one book written at one time, whereas its writings cover a period as long as from Chaucer to our own day.

Again, we read the Bible, or should read it, for a particular purpose—to see how a people of religious genius slowly grew in the knowledge of God, till they reached a conception which Christ could make his own. There is a great deal more in the Bible which is of secondary importance. The scientific ideas of the Jews have no greater claim on our respect than those of any other early people: they were not themselves interested in the subject and have no title to be regarded as experts. When they had laid down the fundamental truth that the world was made by God, it was, naturally and rightly, a matter of comparative indifference to them how He had carried out His plan. To look for scientific teaching in the first chapters of Genesis is as foolish as to look for it in Shakespeare, and for much the same reason.

Once more, the Old Testament contains a great deal of history, but it has no claim to be treated with greater respect than the early records of any other people. Much of it appears, by the best tests which we can apply, to be both accurate and valuable: some of it is demonstrably inaccurate. If anyone is shocked by this statement, he has only to remember that the Old Testament often contains two accounts of the same event, and that both cannot be equally true. The Books of Kings and Chronicles, to take the largest instance, deal with much the same period from a different standpoint, and no historian could doubt that the former is a better historical document. Again, when the kingdoms are divided, no historian will forget that his authorities write from the standpoint of the kingdom of Judah, and that they are naturally prejudiced against the kingdom of Israel. It is a first principle with historians to remember the purpose with which any of their documents are written, and there is no doubt that with the Jews this purpose was always religious. That does not mean that their history or their tradition are without value—on the contrary, they are of the greatest value, quite apart from their supreme literary merit—but it does mean that their main

33   c

interest for us lies, as has been already said, in seeing how their knowledge of God grows with the centuries.

From this point of view the Old Testament is of absorbing interest. We see their conceptions of Jehovah growing from the idea of a powerful God protecting His own tribe till they become sure that He is more powerful than any other God; we see them gradually feeling their way to the belief, first, that He controls other deities, and then to the belief that He is the only God who exists. We see Him thought of first as a God who can be trusted to punish the heathen and secure the supremacy of His own people, and then dimly realized as a God who cares equally for all mankind. In the same way we see the conception of His character changing. He is never merely powerful as the gods of the heathen were, but always just: but it is only slowly that His subjects come to realize that He is supremely loving. In the early books He is human in the lower sense of the word: He orders cruel vengeance and rejoices in the downfall of His enemies. By the end of the book He is seen to be exalted not only "far above all gods," but far above all human weaknesses, and can only be fitly described in the great phrase, "the High and Holy One who inhabiteth eternity."

Some people, no doubt, will be inclined to

say that this is nothing but Evolution, or the natural development of an idea; but, apart from the fact that ideas are not evolved of themselves, we have to remember that hardly any people except the Jews have ever come of themselves to that belief in one God which seems to us so necessary. There was one king of Egypt who reached this belief and tried to force it on his people, but he had no disciples and his work died with him, while that of Moses lived. The only real exception among the peoples of the ancient world is to be found in Greece.

But it is very interesting to contrast the entirely different way in which this idea of monotheism, or the existence of one supreme God, came into existence among these two races. The Greeks were a people of very acute brains, who were always anxious to inquire into the causes of things and were not satisfied till they got an answer. When they inquired into the causes of natural events they could not be satisfied with the idea that different gods caused different events—so that one, for instance, was responsible for the day and another for the night, or one for the harvest and another for the vintage. It seemed to them, as thinkers, that there must be one ultimate Cause for everything, and so their philosophers abandoned the popular worship of many gods, and taught that there was only one God behind the world, though they did not profess to know very much about His character.

What happened in Palestine was very different. The Jews were not great thinkers, and they did not arrive at their conclusion by any process of deep thought. If you want to see how they came to believe in one God and to know what He was like, you cannot do better than read some of the book of Amos, who was the first prophet to write down his own message, and whose book is one of the most remarkable in the Bible. He is very anxious to tell you that he was not a "professional" prophet: he was a shepherd, and not a learned man or a trained thinker. But he says quite simply that he heard God speaking to him and that he had no alternative except to hand on the message. "The Lord God hath spoken: who can but prophesy?" So at great personal risk he delivered the message which had been given to him, and his description of God marks an epoch. Listen to one of his sayings: "Lo, he that formeth the mountains and createth the wind, and declareth unto man what is his thought, that maketh the morning darkness, and treadeth upon the high places of the earth, the Lord, the God of hosts, is his name."

Besides these great descriptions of God's majesty, he had much to say of His character.

He told the Jews what, as we have already said, they were very unwilling to believe—that they were not God's "favourites"[1]; and he told them, what everyone finds it very hard to remember, that God does not care for mere worship so much as for loyal service. There was a great deal more still to be learnt, but Amos laid the foundations well and truly, and you have to ask yourself how this unlettered man came by this great knowledge. There is, as far as I know, no other explanation than the one which he gave himself—namely, that God spoke to him, that he was literally inspired. No doubt it is very possible to deceive yourself and to believe that you have heard the voice of God when you have not: the ultimate test must be whether the things you hear are both new and true. Amos passes these tests triumphantly; and it is because of him, and other prophets like him, that we believe that the Jews were the recipients of a special message from God, and that until Jesus Christ came, born, as it was natural he should be, of this chosen people, the greatest revelation of God that had been given to the world is to be found in the Old Testament.

[1] On the contrary, he taught them exactly the opposite: "You only have I known of all the families of the earth: therefore I will visit upon you all your iniquities." This should be enough to destroy the "favouritism" theory once for all.

IV

The Revelation through Jesus Christ

WE have seen that God reveals Himself in many ways, and that a great revelation of Himself was given to and through the Jewish people. The Christian belief is that His revelation was consummated, or made complete, by the coming to earth of the Son of God, born as a Jew, and living a human life on earth. This is such a tremendous belief that it is not surprising that many people find it hard to accept; but if we believe in the existence of God and, further, believe that man is made in His image—that is to say, is more "divine" than anything else that He has made—it would seem, as we say, "natural" that if God wishes to reveal Himself it should be by some such method. The fact that other religions, besides the Christian, have similar stories of incarnations, or of gods coming down to dwell as men and among men, show how natural the idea is, and so far from being an argument against Christianity is really a support to it. No one supposes that the whole nature and character of God can be perfectly shown in one human life, but it is reasonable to suppose that a human life is the best way in which they can be shown. We have then to look at the life of Christ and see (just as we did in the case of the Jewish prophets) whether the message which he gave, both by word and action, seems to justify the claims which are made for it.

But before we do that we must consider in what form the message comes to us. As has been said already, Christ did not write anything himself, so that the message comes to us at second-hand, and that is why so much time is spent over the "criticism" of the four gospels —that we may satisfy ourselves whether the report given is one which we can trust. Three of our gospels are very closely connected, and it is certain that much of them was written very soon after our Lord's death: St. John's gospel was written later, and by one who had meditated for many years on the things which he had heard and seen. The pictures which they give naturally differ a good deal in detail —sometimes they seem to be consciously correcting one another and sometimes they are emphasizing points which the others seem to have passed over lightly—but there is no doubt that they are all trying to give an honest picture, or that the portraits which they draw are consistent with one another in their main features. The differences are like those which exist between the portraits of different artists, each with a style of his own.

So far as the story goes, they are all in agreement. A child, Jesus, was born in the reign of the emperor Augustus, and lived in Nazareth.[1] We are told hardly anything of his early days until he came in contact with the last of the great prophets, John the Baptist. He was baptized by him, and soon afterwards we find him preaching, at first probably in Galilee, near his home, and afterwards in Jerusalem. His preaching and the wonderful works which he performs in healing the sick make everyone anxious to hear him, and at the same time alarm the religious authorities, who think that his teaching is contrary to theirs. He gathers round him a small band of devoted disciples, who gradually come to believe that he is the Messiah or King whom all pious Jews expected: he tells them that they are right, and takes them with him on his last journey to

[1] I have omitted the story of the virgin birth because that is not found in all the gospels. It would be a mistake to argue that Christ must be the Son of God because he was born of a virgin, but it is perfectly reasonable to argue that if he was in truth the Son of God his coming into the world would be unlike that of other men. The gospels do not use the story as evidence for his divinity, which makes it all the more reasonable to accept it.

Jerusalem, where he and they know that they will be in great danger from the hostility of the priests. The high priests, who were Sadducees, and the Pharisees, who were the special guardians of the law which they thought he was encouraging people to break, are so frightened that they appeal to the Roman governor to have him put to death, saying that he claimed to be the Son of God. Pilate is not much interested in this charge; but finally, fearing a riot which would be discreditable to him, consents to crucify him. His disciples forsake him, and think at first when he dies that all is over, but on the third day they become convinced that he has risen from the dead. All their old faith in him came back, and from that moment they were quite fearless in proclaiming not only that he was the Messiah, but that he was in very truth what his enemies had accused him of claiming to be, the Son of God. The Christian Church had begun.

As will be seen, there is only one point in this story which is difficult to accept, and that is the story of the Resurrection. On that there are two things to be said. In the first place, mankind has always found it very hard to believe that life comes to an end when the body dies; and, though the belief in a future life takes very different forms, there are few people who do not share it in some form or other. This strong feeling may be said to create a presumption in its favour; and when we see how little the things which happen to the body need affect the life of the soul or destroy the character, which is the really important thing about a man, it is hard to believe that one particular kind of bodily disaster can mean the destruction of the whole man. Things which are really good do not seem to perish, and the goodness of a good character seems to us to be the most real thing in the world. In the second place, so far as the resurrection of Christ is concerned, we should realize that the evidence is as good as it can be. If the disciples had been expecting something of the kind it would be easy to say that they persuaded themselves it had happened; but we have their own word for it that it was the very last thing which they dared to hope for. They were absolutely beaten men, when *something happened* which changed them into the fearless preachers of Christ whom we meet in the Acts. It is very certain that they were entirely persuaded of the fact that Christ was still alive, and very difficult to doubt that their story is true.

It hardly need be said how important this point is. If God had allowed Christ to die upon the cross it would have looked as if the powers of evil were strong enough to .destroy utterly the best of men, and our belief in a good God would have been very seriously shaken. From our point of view it was "natural" that God should save the world from this mistake, and should show once for all at this supreme moment that He is Lord not only of life, but of death, and that goodness cannot perish utterly. It was impossible for death to conquer, for that would have meant the final triumph of evil in God's world. St. Peter was quite right when he said that "God raised him up, having loosed the pains of death: because *it was not possible* that he should be holden of it."[1]

Similarly, when we look at the picture which we are given of the character of Christ the agreement between our writers is equally clear. There is no sort of doubt either of the kind of life which Jesus lived or as to the general nature of the example which he set to his followers. The first word which occurs to us is "unselfish": it is impossible to think of him as seeking any advantage for himself or as using his wonderful powers for his own advantage (which is what the devil tempted him to do). He used them always to help other people, whether they were friends or strangers, and he died under torture with words of forgiveness to his enemies on his lips. His is the only character in history to which it is possible to

[1] See Note A at end of chapter.

43

apply the word "perfect," and even those who are not Christians have sometimes adopted the rule of trying so to live that Christ would approve their actions: and it makes the same appeal to people of every race and of every century.

Now this picture of Christ's life and character is given to us by people who were not specially gifted, and who often confess in their narrative that they did not understand what he meant; several times they tell us of foolish questions which they asked, and of the way in which he had to set them right. It is quite impossible that they should have invented such a character, even if that kind of imaginative writing had been known in their day. There is therefore every reason to believe that their account is true, and that Christ really did and said the things which they report of him.

But we are trying to look at Christ not simply as he was in himself, but as a revelation of God; for we believe that he came into the world not only to show what men should be, but also what God's nature was, and this he did in two ways. In the first place, he lived his whole life in the closest touch with God: he never seemed to doubt that God was with him, and so he was able from the first to speak with an authority which no other teacher could claim, and to dare, for instance, to rewrite the old Law of Moses, which would have been an incredibly impious thing for a mere Jew to attempt. At every point, and especially in every difficulty, he appealed to God, whom he called his Father, for help and guidance, and he always told his disciples that it was through this help and guidance that he performed his mighty works. Now it is of course possible that he was mistaken, but it would be very strange indeed if a perfectly good life was lived on a perfectly mistaken theory; so that the first thing which we learn from him about God is the kind of life on which He looks with favour, and the kind of help which He gives to those who ask Him.

But those who knew Jesus felt that this was not enough to say of him. They felt that his touch with God was so close that he must be himself divine. They were gradually feeling their way to this belief when they called him Messiah; and when they knew that he had risen from the dead they no longer had any doubts left, for they felt that God had proclaimed him as His own Son by conquering death in his person. And so they sought out different words in which to describe his relationship to God, for all words are only metaphors or pictures, and no one word could fully describe anything so wonderful. Some-

45

times they called him "the Son," but that suggests that he was in some way subordinate to God as earthly sons are to their parents; sometimes they called him "the Word" to suggest that he perfectly expressed the will of God, as a man's words express his character, and sometimes they called him "the picture of the invisible God," which means that he gave on earth, so far as it could be given in one short life, the truest possible representation of what God is.[1]

This last phrase is perhaps the simplest and the best: in any case, it sums up what we have been trying to show—that by studying Christ's life we shall get the truest idea which it is possible for man to form of God's real character. You have only to think for a moment to see what light this throws on the question, and how impossible it makes some of the theories which men have held of the way in which God might act. You cannot conceive of Christ as being cruel or capricious or unjust, but a great many religions have thought, and still think, of their gods as showing all these qualities. There is a great deal about God which we do not know, but ever since Christ came there have been some things which we think we know with certainty. When a missionary goes to heathen countries he goes

[1] See Note B at end of chapter.

with the gospel, which means "good news," and the great good news which he takes is that God may be rightly described as our Almighty and Most Merciful Father. It is unnecessary to show what a vast difference that must make to those who have been accustomed to think of Him as a Powerful and Unforgiving Master. And this is the gospel of Christ, based, as he always said, on the knowledge which the Jewish prophets had reached, but expanded and developed by him in teaching which a child can understand, and ratified and confirmed by God Himself, by the guidance given to Jesus throughout his earthly life and by the supreme testimony of his resurrection from the dead.

NOTE A

So far as our life after death is concerned, the doctrine of the resurrection is made difficult for many people by a misunderstanding of the phrase "the resurrection of the body." We have St. Paul's authority for interpreting this as meaning "a spiritual body" and, whatever that great phrase may mean, it clearly rules out a resurrection of the flesh. What the Christian doctrine wishes to safeguard is the personality, which, with our present knowledge, we can only conceive in a bodily shape. If there were such a word as "recognizability" it would suggest the idea which the words in the creed are intended to convey: Christ was recognized by his disciples, but his risen "body" was not identical with that which hung on the Cross.

47

NOTE B

Another great phrase is that contained in the Nicene Creed, where Christ is called Light of Light, which means, of course, light proceeding from light, *lumen de lumine*. If we consider the relation between what we call "sunlight" on earth, and the sun from which it comes, we shall have another valuable metaphor in our minds. It is perfectly real sunlight, often as much as earth can bear, and in the same way Christ's revelation of God was a perfectly real revelation of God, conditioned by the circumstances of his earthly life.

V

The Beginnings of Christian Organization

WE have seen how the Christian Church came into existence: it was a body of men united to proclaim the view of God and man which Christ had taught. At first they did not trouble themselves greatly either about elaborating their doctrines or about perfecting their organization: we must remember that, through a mistaken interpretation of their Master's words, many believed that the end of the world was very soon to come. So far as doctrines went they were content with the simple creed that "Jesus is Lord," which carried with it a belief in all that he had said: in the speeches of theirs which we read in the Acts we see how they tried to convince their fellow Jews that he was in truth the Messiah whom the prophets had foretold, and the fulfilment of the hopes of their nation. As for organization, they were content with the simple ceremony of baptism to initiate their converts, and encouraged all who were baptized to try and live as Christ himself had lived: they celebrated the Eucharist, and they observed "the Lord's Day": they tried in Jerusalem the experiment of "having all things in common," remembering how little he had cared to claim any possessions for himself, but the experiment was not successful, and the Christians in Jerusalem had soon to be supported by contributions from outside.

At first, as was not unnatural for Jews, even for Christian Jews, they tried to keep their new knowledge to their own people, and it was only after a good deal of disputing that they agreed that people of other nations, "gentiles," could be admitted to the Christian society: much of St. Paul's early life was taken up with the struggle to have them admitted as equals. When this had once been accepted, the Christian doctrines began to spread rapidly outside Palestine, and especially in Asia Minor and Greece. It was a great moment in the history of the Christian Church when St. Paul made up his mind, as a result of his vision of the man of Macedonia, to cross over into Europe: it was quite possible that he might have decided that a religion born in Asia was better suited for Asiatics, but he was himself a Roman citizen and saw that to work towards Rome was the right strategic plan. It is quite clear that the existence of the Roman Empire, which had brought peace to the world, and by its great roads had made travel easy for the first time, gave a great opportunity for the preachers of a new faith.

But as time went on it became clear that the world was not so soon to come to an end: Paul's earliest epistles (to the Thessalonians) show him correcting this belief, which he once shared: and this meant that the Church must do three things. It must arrange for a permanent record of what Christ did and said: it must define more accurately what was the Christian belief, and lastly it must arrange an organization which could keep its growing numbers together; for the Church was beginning to include people of different races and different ways of thought, and people of a new generation to whom Christ was becoming a figure of past history. Those three problems resulted in course of time in the creation of the New Testament, in the definition of the creeds and in the development of the Christian ministry: all three were of slow growth and it was not for several generations that all were reached, but it will be most convenient to consider them now.

The first is the easiest to explain, for it is a mere matter of history. It soon became clear that some account of Christ's life must be given, and by the end of the first century our four Gospels had been written, the first three, as has already been said, having come into existence a good deal earlier. It is possible that each of them represents the tradition held in one of the great cities, St. Matthew, for instance, being mainly read at Antioch and St. John at Ephesus. There were many other authorities, as we can see from the first verses of St. Luke, but about halfway through the second century our four gospels were accepted as authoritative. Again, the need was soon felt for an account of the earliest days of the Church, and St. Luke carried on his story in the Acts: it is probable that he meant to write a third volume, but we have no evidence that he did so; in any case his second volume, the Acts, was an authoritative history of its earliest years. Then Christians naturally held in great honour anything that had been written by the Apostles, and so we get that large section of the New Testament which is called Epistles. These were generally letters written to particular churches dealing with particular points of difficulty, but sometimes they were addressed to particular groups of churches or to the Church as a whole, and were meant to be read aloud to the assembled congregation. They were treasured by the Churches which possessed them, and it was natural to include them in any collection of sacred Christian writings. Lastly there were prophetic writings, such as the Jews had composed before Christ's time, and one such Christian book, the Revelation, was finally included. By the end of the second century there was a very general agreement as to what should be regarded as the Christian sacred books, and after long discussion on minor points our present New Testament was definitely accepted by the end of the fourth century: St. Athanasius and St. Jerome were the two leaders who had most to do with the result.

This was a very great gain, for it produced a book to which those in doubt could refer with certainty, but the danger was that it seemed to set these books quite apart from any others and to prevent people from reading them naturally. It is much easier to quote texts from an inspired book than to read them in their context and see what the author meant, and some Christians have been inclined to use them in this way. It is a great mistake, especially in the case of epistles which were written, as has been said, not as general statements but to meet particular difficulties. Again it is a mistake to suppose that the inspiration of the New Testament is of a totally different kind from that of other books: and lastly it is a worse mistake still to suppose that the Old and New Testaments form one volume of equal authority, and to make Christians responsible for the view of God held by the Jews many centuries before Christ came. But in the last hundred years these dangers have been disappearing and it is becoming easier to read the New Testament as what it is —a book in which the person of Jesus Christ and the teaching of his greatest apostles are set forth honestly and fully by men striving to write under the influence of the Holy Spirit.

The second necessity was to define what Christian people ought to believe. There was no question about their believing the facts of Christ's life and death and resurrection, but it was also necessary to put into words Christ's relationship to God the Father of which, as we have seen, they had at first given various accounts which were rather meant as illustrations than as definitions. Another equally difficult question was to explain how Christ could be both human and divine—God incarnate, as the early Church firmly believed him to be. If you will think for a moment you will see that both these questions are likely to be impossible to be answered exactly in human language, both because we do not know enough and because human language is a very rough instrument. This is so important a point and one so often forgotten that it is worth while to dwell on it. If you try to describe, let us say, fire or a sunset or a piece of music or even some bodily sensation in words you will realize how impossible it is to find words to express what you want to say, and when you are arguing about anything you will find that words get special associations of which it is hard to rid them, so that the same phrase means different things to different people.

If you bear this in mind you will not be surprised that the early Christians found it very difficult to find the right words for these tremendous subjects, and it was not till the fifth century that our three creeds were agreed upon, and only after very long and bitter controversy. Their authors had to rely on what they could find in the New Testament, and none of its books were written for the purpose of supplying material for a creed: they found sayings of Christ which were hard to reconcile with one another, as for instance when he says in one place "the Father is greater than I" and in another "I and the Father are one." It is very much to their credit that they did not try and explain things away, or declare that one view must be false and another true: this is what heretics do, who "choose" one point of view and refuse to admit any other: they tried their best to understand, and when they could not understand left the point as a mystery which their present knowledge did not allow them to comprehend.[1]

It is very easy to sneer at them for their failure to make everything perfectly clear, but

[1] See Note at end of chapter.

any great man of science will tell you that the most dangerous thing for knowledge is when some view is made "an article of faith" on insufficient grounds: he is content to say that he believes a great many things which he cannot either explain or prove, and the "mysteries" of science are quite as numerous and as difficult as any in the Christian creeds. Professor Huxley said that the "necessary antinomies" or contradictions in science were quite as serious as any which Christians had to face, and modern scientists say much the same.

Another reason for gratitude is that the authors of the Apostles' and the Nicene creeds did not try to explain things in the philosophical language of their own day: philosophies and philosophical language are always changing as knowledge grows and it is a very dangerous thing for a Church to pin its faith to one of them. We have an example of this in our Prayer Book in the Athanasian Creed as it is called (though it is really not a creed but a hymn and certainly was not written by St. Athanasius). Everything in that creed is capable of explanation and much that is in it is of great value, but, largely because it is written in a technical language which we have ceased to use, it conveys a quite false impression to the ordinary unlearned person, and it is a very good thing that it has ceased to be used in the ordinary services of the Church. We shall discuss later the position which creeds hold, or ought to hold, in the Christian life; for the present our object is to show how and when the Church accomplished the second of its tasks, the definition of Christian belief.

The third task was to arrange for the organization and discipline of the Christian communities. This took a shorter time to settle, and by the end of the second century the various churches were each controlled by a bishop whose name really means "overseer": he was the undisputed head of his community, but of course he was expected to act in harmony with the other bishops and in accordance with general Christian principles as they were established.

We can see the beginnings of the episcopate in the New Testament, especially in the pastoral epistles, but there appears to have been a period during which the "bishop" was, in some churches at any rate, only one among the presbyters or elders, presiding over them, but not holding permanently a higher rank. It is impossible to follow accurately the history of Christian organization in the second century and it seems probable that the practice varied in different churches, but it is certain that by the end of that century what is called the "monarchical" episcopate was universally established and that it was never questioned during the controversies of the next thousand years. It cannot be historically proved that any bishops are the direct descendants of the Apostles, in the sense that they consecrated the first bishop and that there has been no break since, but it is quite certain that our bishops do trace their consecration back in a direct line for at least 1,700 years, and that is a tradition long enough to command respect.

The controversies which have arisen on the subject are twofold. On the one side there are those who say, quite truly, that the institution of bishops, in the modern sense, cannot be traced with certainty to Our Lord and his apostles. They claim that a "presbyterian" form of government is more primitive and more Christian and that the claims that are made for the authority of bishops are exaggerated. The answer to this is that, whatever may have been the practice for a hundred years, the Church very soon decided in favour of government by bishops, and that whether or not their authority can be traced back to the very highest source—which must always remain a matter of doubt—they have so long a history behind them that the Church could never now be united on any other basis of government.

The other controversy is of the opposite kind. The Church of Rome maintains that Christ intended his Church to have a permanent visible head, who should rule it in his name, and that this position belongs to the Bishop of Rome as the successor of St. Peter. The claim rests on the doubtful interpretation of a saying of Christ's and on a doubtful tradition which makes Peter Bishop of Rome. It is enough to say that nothing seems to have been known of it during the early Christian centuries. Rome was so much the greatest city of the ancient world that its bishop naturally carried great weight; his opinions were sometimes right and sometimes wrong, but it was a long time before it occurred to him or to anyone else to regard his views as infallible, even when he claimed to be expressing the mind of the whole Church. Those who do not accept the Roman Catholic claims are content to refer in the first place to the New Testament which, with the doubtful exception already mentioned, gives no sort of countenance to such a view, and to the evidence of history, which shows not only that no such claims were made for many centuries but that the record of the Roman See since it has asserted them is by no means consistent with infallibility or even with any special possession of Divine inspiration.

We are content, then, to say that Christ left his followers without any definite instructions as to its future organization. The Apostles during their lifetime naturally had a claim to authority, and they handed it on, though naturally with some diminution, to those whom they themselves appointed: as time went on the Church had to develop its own method of government and did so in a little more than a hundred years. It is reasonable to suppose that so general an agreement was not reached without the guidance of the Holy Spirit and we may accept episcopal government as having behind it not only the authority of many Christian centuries but a higher authority still.

NOTE

The doctrine of the Trinity affords the best example of the way in which they dealt with such mysteries. They felt that they must accept Christ's authority and saw that he spoke of the Father, of Himself and of the Spirit as in a sense the same and in a sense different (see for instance John xiv and xv). They did not profess to understand exactly what he meant, but they were sure that they must not try to explain it away. They left it as a mystery, whereas the heretics "chose" interpretations which did not really cover the whole ground. We do not profess to understand it either, but we know enough to be thankful that they did not try to force on the world an explanation based on their very imperfect knowledge. The Athanasian Creed is often criticized as an attempt to explain, whereas it is really a proclamation of a mystery, with (very harsh) denunciation of those who claim to have explained it. If an "explanation" is ever forthcoming it will perhaps be given in terms of psychology, a science of which they could have known nothing. In the meantime it is good for us to have to remember that the nature of God is likely to be beyond our powers both of comprehension and of expression.

VI

The History of the Christian Church

THERE are two great landmarks in the history of the Christian Church: the conversion of the Roman emperor Constantine early in the fourth century and the Reformation in the sixteenth. The first period is that in which the Christians are struggling for their existence, sometimes tolerated by the authorities, sometimes harassed by them and sometimes definitely persecuted. The chief reason why some of the emperors, who allowed all other religions to exist unchecked, tried to destroy the Christian Church was that Christians were thought to be disloyal, because they had a King of their own whom they were bound to obey more than any earthly emperor. The Roman emperors, after the time of Augustus, came more and more to be worshipped as divine, especially in the East, and, though this caused no difficulty to polytheists, it was impossible for a Christian to offer incense to the emperor. This led to many persecutions and many martyrdoms, especially when Christians, though they might be willing to serve in the army, refused to take any oath which spoke of the emperor as God. A further reason for their unpopularity (as we can see in the Acts) was that by declaring all heathen gods to be unreal and their worship useless they tended to throw out of employment all the people who in one way or another got their living from the service of the temples.

The worst periods of persecution were in the third century when two emperors, Decius and Diocletian, definitely tried to stamp Christianity out. The persecutions did not last very long, but they were very violent for a time, sometimes aiming at killing all the Christian officers, especially the bishops, and sometimes at destroying all their sacred books. There are many stories of Christian martyrdoms, for during about two hundred years they had no protection from the law and were at the mercy of any Roman governor who chose to enforce it against them; he was often encouraged to do so by the common people who thought, or pretended to think, that their secret services were a cover for terrible crimes. During all this period it must have seemed very unlikely that Christianity could ever become the State religion: in fact a great writer in the second century uses the phrase "If the emperors should become Christians" as a synonym for impossibility.

But all this time the Christian body was growing and spreading, and, as has been said, at the beginning of the fourth century the emperor Constantine not only adopted the religion himself, but did his best to impose it upon his people. Opinions differ as to his motives: some think that he was genuinely converted, perhaps as a result of a vision which promised him victory in a great battle, others that he was a statesman who saw that Christianity was the only religion which could unite the empire: the truth probably lies somewhere between the two. Opinions differ also as to whether his adoption of Christianity was a good or a bad thing for the Christian Church. It was, of course, a very wonderful triumph that a tiny body starting from an obscure province should in less than three hundred years become the spiritual masters of the whole civilized world, but it is clear that their success brought great dangers with it. It meant that instead of its being dangerous to be a Christian it was even a definite worldly advantage, and that meant that many professed Christianity without really caring about it: again, as the emperor was clearly a very important person, it meant that the Church would be tempted to pay too much attention to his wishes: and lastly it meant that the rulers of the Church would have the opportunity of riches and power and influence, which, as their Master had told them, are very dangerous things. In the long history of the second period we shall see, only too often, how the Church and its rulers yielded to all three temptations.

The second period is a very long one, covering some twelve hundred years, and it is only possible to call attention to a few of its most prominent features. Christianity had not been established as the official religion of the Roman empire for more than a hundred years when that empire began to come to an end, and by the end of the fifth century it only survived in Constantinople and the East: the rest of Europe had been overrun by hordes of barbarians who had destroyed the old system of government and were busy constructing new kingdoms of their own. The bishops, who remained at their posts, were often the only representatives of the old régime, and it is impossible not to wonder what would have happened if they had not been there: Constantine's conversion had been only just in time.

As it was, they were able to maintain some standard of civilization, and in course of time all the barbarian tribes were converted, at any rate in name: it is easy to blame the Christian bishops and missionaries for being too ready to accept converts who were not genuine but perhaps only followed their chief, but this should not blind us to the greatness of their achievement. The result was that the Church received a great many more nominal followers, and the bishops found themselves connected as advisers with barbarian princes who were even less instructed Christians than some of the Roman emperors had been.

Out of this very confused situation there emerged in the ninth and tenth centuries what we are accustomed to call the Holy Roman Empire. It represented a very great idea, that while the emperor looked after the temporal affairs of men the Pope, as the greatest of Christian bishops, should look after their souls, and that the two together should exercise an authority directly given by God and extending over the whole of Christendom. Unfortunately the great idea was never realized in practice. To begin with, there was always a large body of Christian people who were outside this empire and neither recognized the emperor as their master nor the Pope as having a right to speak as their mouthpiece: these were the subjects of the Eastern empire, the direct heir of the emperor of Rome who ruled at Constantinople, and considered their patriarch to have an authority parallel to that of the Pope. Again, the popes and emperors were very seldom able to agree on the precise line of division between the temporal and spiritual concerns of men, for popes always claimed some temporal power and emperors always claimed some voice in spiritual matters, especially in the appointments of bishops. Finally, it was very rare to find either an emperor or a pope who cared solely for the good of Christendom and not at least as much for his own power and glory.

For these various reasons the period of the undisputed supremacy of Christianity was by no means as glorious as it should have been: there were continual quarrels between Church and State, such as that between William Rufus and Anselm, or Henry II and Becket, and the only Pope who suggested a real solution, that the clergy should abandon all their temporal power (Pope Paschal in A.D. 1111) was compelled by his cardinals to withdraw it at once. Because of this state of hostility Christendom was unable to unite against its enemies the Mahommedans, who had become active in the seventh century, and in spite of much valour, such as that shown by the Crusaders, were able to overrun much Christian land, such as Palestine, North Africa and Spain, and finally to take Constantinople itself in the year 1453.

It was this general failure of the Church to make the most of its opportunities which led in the sixteenth century to the epoch-making event which we call the Reformation, but there were many minor causes which contributed to it. The nations of Europe were becoming more self-conscious and less willing to think of themselves merely as part of the empire, and indeed the empire had for some three centuries been little more than a name. Greek scholarship, especially after the fall of Constantinople, was rediscovered, and what is called the New learning, though most of it is really old, came just at the time when the invention of printing enabled it to spread rapidly. The Papacy had fallen very low in men's minds as a religious institution: in the fourteenth century the Popes had been mere creatures of France, and in the fifteenth many of them had been anything but Christian in their lives. They commanded very little respect and were merely thought of as scheming Italian princes.

The immediate cause which produced the explosion was that a Pope, anxious to raise money for the building of St. Peter's, authorized preachers to collect it by selling "indulgences," which were something very like a pardon for sins. This roused the indignation of Martin Luther in Germany, and when the Pope tried to repress him by force he found that he could not do it even with the emperor's help. Most of Northern Europe threw off its allegiance to the Pope and the formal unity of Christendom was definitely broken.[1]

The inevitable result was that different churches grew up in the different countries which disowned the authority of Rome, and that, though they all agree in accepting the Christian creeds, they have insisted on minor points of doctrine in a way which prevents them from acting cordially together. Some, for instance, have disowned the doctrine of episcopacy, and some went so much further than others in the reaction from Rome that they have parted with other doctrines and practices which were sound in themselves but had been misused under Roman authority. The Church of England, with which we are specially concerned, did not altogether escape this mistake, but as it has always appealed not only to the Bible but also to sacred tradition, it can fairly claim that its object was merely to clear away abuses and to recover the true doctrines which had been obscured or for-

[1] It should be remembered that as the Eastern or Greek Church had never accepted the papal claims the unity had not for many centuries been complete.

gotten: but of its position more will be said later.

It will be clear that there is a striking contrast between the third period of Christian history and that which precedes it; Christendom is no longer united as it nominally was, and the disunion is all the greater because in every country where the papal authority has been rejected other societies besides the reformed Church have grown up, so that Christendom presents a very distracted appearance. It is quite true to say that this disunion is very far from the ideal which Christ set before his Church, but there are several reasons why we need not feel that the present situation is either hopeless or altogether deplorable.

In the first place, we must remember that the so-called unity of Christendom was always more nominal than real, so that we have not lost a "golden age" to which we can only look back with regret. In the second place, the unity which was then reached was largely a result of external pressure which stifled freedom of thought, and narrowed religion down to what authority approved. It seems quite clear that what Our Lord cared for most was unity of Spirit, and he could only care for unity of organization so far as it expresses this or fosters it. If we may borrow a metaphor from politics it seems likely that the new unity of Christendom will be reached by a federation of Churches which agree upon the fundamental doctrines of our Church, but each wish to emphasize some particular aspect of the truth. The unity which the Roman Church offers is a much narrower and more external thing, and can only be obtained by accepting its terms, which mean complete submission. It should be plainly said that much as we admire the splendid work which has been and is being done by its members, there is nothing in its past history or in its present policy which makes those terms seem reasonable, and that the appeal which the Reformers made both to tradition and to the Gospels still seems decisive against the papal claim to dominate the Christian world.

NOTE

The reformers emphasized the importance of private judgment as against authority. Though it is quite clear that there is a need of authority there is no doubt that it had been abused and private judgment unduly coerced. To enforce belief can never make for that honesty of mind which Christ demands, and it became a scandal when the force was applied in his name by a power which was not even morally respectable. For the excesses which some reformers undoubtedly committed most of the blame must lie with those who had repressed all freedom of thought, in a spirit far removed from that of the great Fathers of the Church.

VII

The Influence of the Christian Church

WE have so far been considering the external history of the Christian Church and have given as shortly as possible an outline of its record. The history has not been a happy one, for the folly and ambition of men have too often turned it into a merely human society, competing, not always successfully, with other bodies of men for earthly success. But the real work of the Church has always been done in the hearts of men, and if we wish to judge its success we must look not at the amount of territory which it has ruled but at the influence which it has had on men's character and conduct.

Here we shall find that the record is much more glorious. If we believe the Church to be the creation of our Lord Jesus Christ, commissioned to spread his message throughout the world, we cannot help being disappointed that so much remains to be done: there are very large regions of the world in which his gospel has never been preached,

and a very great many Christian countries in
which his teaching is very imperfectly followed,
but this is no reason for not realizing how
much has been accomplished. No Christian
ought to blame those who speak of the Church
as having failed, for we ought to have a
higher standard than anyone else of what it
ought to do, but if we see what has been done
already, and how it has been done, we shall
be encouraged to try to carry the process
further in our own day. The magistrates of
Thessalonica were quite right when they said
that Paul and Silas were trying to "turn the
world upside-down": Christ's teaching was
revolutionary in the proper sense of the word,
for he encouraged everyone to forget himself
and care more for other people, and that is
the greatest revolution which can happen to
any man. We have now to see in what
respects this revolution has been successfully
accomplished.

No doubt the greatest change which Christianity has slowly brought about in the world
is in the respect for human life and the sympathy with suffering of all kinds. In ancient
days, as in many heathen countries still, human
life and human suffering were very little
thought of. Christ taught us that every man
who lives is of infinite value in the sight of
our heavenly Father, and by his attitude

towards the sick and suffering he showed an example for all his disciples to follow. The early Christians were not slow to do this: it was their doing that hospitals of every kind sprang up all over the Roman Empire, and it may truly be said that all such institutions owe their origin to his inspiration. As time goes on, we realize that there are more kinds of cruelty and misery to be attacked and relieved: those who take these tasks in hand often would not call themselves Christians, but they are doing a work which is pre-eminently Christ's, and no one who does claim that name can fail to see that he is bound to sympathize and help as best he can. Sometimes, as in the case of the reform of our prisons, Christian people have taken the lead, and there is no denying that they ought always to have done so, but what is plain is that in all civilized countries the Christian spirit is gradually coming to prevail and that is one of the triumphs of Christianity, and one of the great proofs of its truth.

There is one particular field which is worth considering closely, because it gives an admirable illustration of the way in which Christ's spirit works. You can read through the New Testament without finding any definite condemnation of slavery. Christ never mentioned the subject, and when St. Paul speaks of it he is content to say that Christian masters must treat their slaves as brethren and that Christian slaves must remember that no matter to whom their bodies may belong they are all bond-servants of Christ. It seems to us obvious that it is impossible to treat anyone both as a brother and as a slave, for a slave is a person who has no rights whatever, but it is clear that for many centuries good Christian people failed to draw the obvious conclusion. Sometimes they deluded themselves by thinking that Christian rules did not apply to barbarian races, such as black men, and sometimes they persuaded themselves that slaves were really happier as they were. So slavery went on, getting worse and worse, for the kidnapping of slaves in Africa, and their transportation to America, were worse than anything which had happened in ancient days, until it occurred to some Christian people that to traffic in slaves or even to own them could not be consistent with Christ's law. It is very interesting that as soon as men like Wilberforce put the question in a perfectly straightforward way before the English people the conscience of the nation at once answered it without any hesitation: there was, of course, strong opposition from all those who profited by the trade, but in a very short time, considering how long slavery had gone unquestioned, first the slave trade and then slavery itself were abolished for all British subjects and a large sum of money was paid to secure that slaves should be freed without undue loss to their owners. Other nations more or less readily followed this lead, and any slavery which still exists in Christian countries can only do so by disguising itself as skilfully as possible. It has been said that the action of this country in the matter of slavery forms "one of the few perfectly virtuous pages in the history of nations," but it must never be forgotten that the ultimate credit belongs not so much to the English nation as to the Christianity which they first learnt to apply to this particular problem.

In the same way it is by no means an accident that the position of women is far higher and more secure in Christian countries than in any other. Here again Christ never made any "pronouncement" about the rights of women, but the way in which he treated them showed that he did not accept the view of their inferiority which was, and is, common in many parts of the world. Some of his most faithful followers were women, and his Mother has always been held by Christians in very special honour. The most illuminating story on this subject in the Gospels is that told by St. John of his conversation with the woman of Samaria.

She was of poor position and character and belonged to a despised race, but in the eyes of the disciples the mere fact that she was a woman was enough to make her unfit for their Master's society. "They marvelled," we are told, "that he spoke with a woman," and yet it was with her that he held one of his deepest conversations and to her that he told some of the most spiritual truths in the whole gospel.

It was impossible that this example should not tell, and so it has come about, though there has never been any formal declaration on the subject, that in all Christian countries women are no longer regarded as the inferiors of men. The process of translating this new belief into action has been a slow one and is not yet fully accomplished, but it is becoming clear to all thinking people that the idea that there can be one standard of morals for women and another for men is contrary to all Christ's teaching. After all, St. Paul nearly two thousand years ago said that "in Christ Jesus there could be neither male nor female" but that "all were one in him," and once again we see that the unspoken word of Christ has prevailed among all those who try to follow his teaching, with results to the world which we cannot yet fully estimate.

These two instances are the most conspicuous of those in which Christianity has fulfilled its task of changing the minds of men and making a peaceful but complete revolution in their ways of thought, but there are other spheres too in which it has been active. We said in the last chapter that the barbarians who came into Europe in the fifth century often accepted Christianity without very clearly understanding what it meant, and often without abandoning their own heathen ideas. But we must never forget that it was the Church which gave them whatever civilization they received. The Church was the only Roman institution which was left and through it they learnt the great traditions of Roman law and justice. The Romans had a great love for justice before Christianity appeared, so that it cannot be claimed as a Christian discovery. In this case there was no revolution which needed to be made, but it was the Christian Church which preserved the Roman ideas of justice and government in a world which otherwise would have collapsed in chaos, so that some at least of the credit is justly its due.

Most people know so little history that they think of the monasteries as collections of idle and selfish men which were rightly abolished in this country in the reign of Henry VIII: they forget, if they ever knew, that during the dark ages of European history they performed services which are quite invaluable. They

77

kept up a tradition of learning which would otherwise have perished: they taught the children when there was no one else to teach: they cared for the sick when there were no doctors to relieve them: they fed the destitute when there was no poor-law to keep them from starvation: they worked their estates as good landlords when the land was being harried and neglected: they built great churches which are still an inspiration to those who see them. Whatever their later faults may have been, for no human institution remains at its best for ever, they kept alive a tradition of culture and piety which nothing else could have preserved.

Once more, though it is perfectly true that many popes and other ecclesiastics in the Middle Ages behaved in a very worldly manner, we should not forget that in every country in Europe there were great ecclesiastical statesmen who laboured for justice and good government, and, if many Christians in high places set a lamentable example, there were many others who well deserved the name of saint whose virtues shine out in a dark world. The simplest and greatest example is St. Francis of Assisi who, in a century when the Church was in danger of becoming very worldly, lived wholly in the spirit of Christ and showed that his Master's example was as powerful as it had ever been. It is by lives such as his that the influence of Christianity was spread, and the Church may fairly claim to be judged rather by its saints than by those who rose, by worldly methods and for worldly reasons, to the highest positions in its government.

The function of Christianity has always been to remind men that their highest duty is to God and that if they wish to please Him they will do so best by following the example of Christ. In our earliest period it is easy to see how this task was fulfilled: the heathen world had no proper conception of God or of the duty of a man to his neighbour: the Christians taught the true theory and showed the right practice: it is no mere accident that their enemies said of them in derision: "See how these Christians love one another."

In our second period the task before the Church was no longer to proclaim the true theory, except to the barbarian invaders whom they did convert with great courage and at least partial success: it was rather to keep alive the Christian virtues and to spread them among people who had often accepted the Christian doctrines in a very half-hearted way. There were times when, in this sense, the world seemed more likely to overwhelm Christianity than Christianity to overcome the world, but the tradition was never wholly lost, and from one point of view the Reformation was a determined protest made by Christians against the low standards of morality which their leaders had accepted.

In our third period the twofold task is with us again. The growth of learning and the discoveries of science have made it necessary for us to reconsider and try to restate our Christian beliefs: however difficult this may be, it should not be impossible to those who are sure that all truth must be ultimately consistent with the great Christian doctrines. That is one side of our task as proclaiming the truth, and another is to preach the gospel to the heathen, of whose existence we are much more conscious than were the men of the Middle Ages: there is nothing more encouraging in Christian history than the vast growth in missionary effort of the last hundred years.

When the Church Missionary Society was founded at the beginning of the nineteenth century no English man or woman could be found who was ready to go out to Africa as a missionary, and for many years after that it was definitely forbidden to send missionaries to India. What has been done since that time in Africa, India, China and Japan is little short of amazing: Christian communities with their own native bishops and clergy exist everywhere to prove that our religion is one for the whole world.

And then we have, as always, to try to practise the Christian virtues and to be on the look out for new spheres into which they can be extended. Every form of cruelty and suffering is, or should be, a challenge to the conscience of Christians, and we shall find in the Gospels an unfailing source of instruction and inspiration. There are many to-day who affect to despise the Christian virtues, and if they are to be converted to the truth it can only be by seeing that Christians are making a real effort to practise them. It is easy, and indeed right, to feel contempt for those who profess a creed which they do not try to carry out, and such criticisms are best met not by argument but by showing that we at least are trying to live as Christ would have us live.

VIII

Christian Belief

WHEN we begin to consider the kind of life which Christ would have us live we find that we cannot separate theory and practice, or faith and life. Many people think that it consists in practising what are vaguely called "Christian Virtues," and imply that it does not much matter on what theory this is done. No doubt if it were necessary to choose between leading a good life and holding a true belief, we should all of us choose the former, but as has already been said, the suggestion is absurd: "the better the theory, the better the practice" is a universal rule, of which "the truer the faith the better the life" is only one example. However, as theory comes before practice, we must say something of the Christian faith before we go on to discuss the effect which it ought to have upon our lives.

We have already said something of the Christian belief about God. It cannot be too often said that for us God means the union of absolute power and absolute goodness. About the former there is nothing that can be added to the words of the Nicene Creed— "I believe in God the Father Almighty, Maker of heaven and earth, and of all things visible and invisible": human language cannot go further, and those who speak as if the Christian God was someone too small for the modern mind to accept are talking nonsense, though they may find some excuse for their folly in the petty notions of God with which some Christians are content. But absolute power in itself is only alarming, and not something to be worshipped, still less to be loved. We have continually to remind ourselves that God is for us the source of everything that is beautiful, everything that is true and everything that is good. When we worship Him we are not only worshipping the Father who cares for us all, though we are naturally inclined to think of Him first in this way, but are worshipping also all those great ideas which alone can satisfy the mind of man. The artist believes in a Beauty which he cannot perfectly see, the philosopher or man of science in a Truth which he cannot perfectly find: for the Christian, God means all these things, and we have already discussed the reasons which make us believe in a personal God and not in mere abstract ideas.

It is because God is so much more than our loving Father that Christians should be encouraged to meditate upon His nature: otherwise our religion may become nothing but a general feeling of kindliness to everyone, which is an excellent thing in itself, but does not exercise the whole of our nature. We are bidden to serve Him not only with our heart and soul but also with our mind, and that means that we should try to accustom ourselves to think of all truth and all beauty as showing us more of His character. We are far too ready to think of worship as being merely a matter of prayer, whereas really it should be a lifting up of our hearts in praise. This does not, of course, mean that God is like a King who wishes to hear himself flattered by his subjects: it means that to think of the wonder and beauty of the world, and the glorious fact that we are able in our degree to understand and appreciate it, or to think of the good things that men have been able to do which we can at least admire and try to imitate, leads us on to gratitude and thankfulness and praise to God who made so wonderful a world and has given us the power, possessed by no other creature, to understand and to appreciate it.

The Mahommedans daily recite a form of prayer which the Prophet commanded them to repeat: to us it hardly seems like prayer at all, for it is a recitation of the greatness of God of which they thus continually remind themselves. No doubt the repetition, like all repetitions, is in danger of becoming formal and meaningless, but the idea which Mahomet had in mind is one which Christians too often forget. Their worship may often stop at praise, but ours is too often limited to rather petty and selfish prayer. If they, who really know God almost entirely as Power, feel it right to recall His majesty and greatness so often, surely we who have been taught to think of Him not only as Power but as Love should be even more ready to offer our daily sacrifice of praise and thanksgiving.

For there is no doubt that it was the Love of God of which Christ most encouraged us to think, and that Love is the name by which we can most fittingly call Him: when we say that we believe in God the Father Almighty, we are saying, among other things, that we believe Love to be all-powerful and therefore strong enough to conquer Sin and Death, which are the strongest things which we know. When we love, we are sharing in the nature of God: St. John goes so far as to say that love and life are the same thing. This seems to us at first a mere poetical phrase, but we know so little of what life really is, as distinguished from the processes which keep the body alive, that it may very likely be the exact truth. A man who cannot love has ceased to live in any real sense of the word: though his body may go on performing its functions with perfect regularity, we ought no more to think of him as fully or really alive than we should of a man whose brain has ceased to work, for the power of loving is even more the characteristic possession of the human race than the power of reasoned thought.

We think of God, then, as being Almighty, and as perfect in love as in power, and we at once find ourselves faced with the problem of the evil in the world. And here, if we are wise, we shall confess that we are unable to give a full answer to the question. There are many things which we can truly and profitably say. Much of the suffering in the world is of the nature of a warning, without which it would be hardly possible for life to continue to exist: much of it is quite clearly the result of human folly and human sin, and if we are asked why human folly and human sin are allowed to exist it is a perfectly fair answer that they were bound to exist if man was to be a really free agent, and that if he was not he was not worth the trouble of creation. All man's greatness comes from his power to choose between two alternatives, and there could be no conceivable glory in choosing right if it was impossible to choose wrong.

All these things are true and they cover a great deal of the ground, but they do not cover it all. We know too little about the animal creation to speak of it with certainty, and it is very possible that we exaggerate the sufferings of animals, but it is very difficult to connect what we do know with the unfailing love of God. The most we can say is that for the evil which we do most certainly know, which is Sin, we can see an answer and a remedy and that we believe that there must be a similar solution for everything else which seems to thwart the loving will of God. We must therefore consider what is the Christian doctrine about sin.

In the first place, we must get out of our heads the idea that mankind is punished because of an offence committed by its earliest ancestors. Even if the earliest Hebrews had believed this it would be no part of our faith, and as a matter of fact it would seem that they did not, for the sin of Adam, which on this theory had such tremendous consequences, is never mentioned again throughout the Old Testament. They knew that they were telling a great story, or myth, to show the true nature of sin and did not think that they were narrating actual history. The moral of the story, as we can see, is that primitive man lives at first without knowing the difference between right and wrong: when he eats the forbidden tree he receives the knowledge of good and evil. He discovers two things: first, that there is such a thing as sin; and secondly, that he has a kinship with God, for to know the difference between right and wrong is a divine quality. It is a pity that this process is always spoken of as "the Fall," which is to fix the attention on only one side of it. The power to do evil and the power to do good are different sides of the same capacity, just as we have already seen that if a man possesses the priceless gift of freewill he must be able to misuse his freedom.

If we look at the story of the Fall from this point of view, we see that it is a pictorial statement of what is quite clearly a fact of evolution, for if man was developed from the lower animals there must have been a moment when he acquired this capacity which he had not possessed before. And if we look closely at the story we shall see how it shows us all the characteristic qualities of sin as we know it: there is the desire to break a law merely for the sake of breaking it: there is the desire to gratify the senses, and the desire for power: and when the offence has been committed there is the sense of shame and the

Christian Belief

attempt to put the blame on someone else, with both of which we are only too familiar in our own case. The primary fact about us is that, just as we are capable of being so much nobler than any other creature, so we are capable of becoming infinitely worse, for the deliberate cruelty and selfishness of a human being is far worse than the same quality shown instinctively by a beast.

Mankind, then, is sin-ful, in the literal sense that we are by the very fact of our nature, all liable to sin; it is often forgotten that we are also grace-ful in exactly the same sense, that we all have the capacity for realizing what is right and trying to do it. In the course of human history the failure of man became more obvious than his success, and the question inevitably arose What was God's attitude towards this failure? The first and most natural thought is that He must be very angry, for man knows all the time that he is consciously doing wrong and if he finds it difficult to make excuses for himself, or to forgive himself, how can he expect God to forgive? We see at once that everything must depend upon our view of the character of God. If He is merely like a man, only infinitely more powerful, there can be no hope: He will not forgive and will punish with a punishment which is terrible in proportion to His power. So we find that, where the view of God is low, mankind is tortured with fears of inevitable and well-deserved punishment.

As we have already seen, the Jews went through the primitive stages of religion, and suffered from this kind of fear, but their glory is that they passed through them into a nobler and truer view. Hosea was perhaps the first of their prophets to tell them of the infinite forgiveness of God, and his story of how God told him to forgive his sinful wife is an anticipation of that other story which Christ told about the forgiveness of the Prodigal Son. For Christians there is no excuse for starting with the idea that God's first instinct is to be angry: the parable which I have just mentioned, and indeed all Christ's teaching, gives us a very different view from that. God is love, and His first feeling towards His sinful children must be that of sorrow, coupled with a desire to forgive if and when forgiveness is possible. He must wish us to return into a proper relationship with Him.

But we know very well from our own experience that forgiveness is not quite a simple matter. If anyone is forgiven before he realizes that he has done wrong and before he is really sorry, the forgiveness may do more harm than good, and we cannot put the matter more simply than to say that Christ came into the world for these reasons—to make us see where we had gone wrong, to make us feel sorry for it, and thereby to make it possible for us to live as children of God. Any idea of the "Atonement" which suggests that God was angry and had to be appeased is entirely unChristian, especially if it suggests, as Milton does in *Paradise Lost*, that Christ was more kindly disposed to the world than God the Father. The Christian doctrine is that "God so loved the world that He gave His only begotten Son" to enable us to live "at one" with Him, and if we ask how Christ's life and death bring this about, the answer is not difficult, if we put away the thoughts suggested by difficult words like Atonement and Propitiation: the sufferings of Christ on the Cross show the evil of the world doing its worst to perfect goodness: there is an amazing prophecy of Plato that if a perfect man came into the world he would be crucified, and that prophecy is literally fulfilled. It is impossible to read the story without hating the sin which caused it: it is said that when the barbarian king Clovis first heard the story he cried out "Why was I not there with my Franks?" and all of us must have felt something of the same emotion. We realize what sin is and what it inevitably does, and we see clearly on which side we want to be. So long as we look at the story of the Crucifixion merely as an event in history we shall be tempted to think that we should not have committed such a terrible crime ourselves: but if we look more deeply we see that the motives which influenced the chief priests and Pilate and even Judas are the same motives which are constantly appealing to us and we see the shame of yielding to them. The "salvation" or "redemption" which we preach is not the passive acceptance of something done for us in which we have no share. To those who ask what we mean when we speak of Christ as the Saviour of the world, our answer will be that "Christ's love redeems the world by creating the conditions in which righteousness and love can be all-powerful." [1]

Christ never explained the "problem" of sin any more than he explained the "problem" of suffering, but just as he showed both how our own sufferings could be borne and the sufferings of others relieved, so he showed us the true nature of sin and the way to resist it. And above all he showed us God's attitude towards the frailty of men, both in his own continual compassion and in his supreme cry upon the Cross: "Father, forgive them, for they know not what they do." In that cry we have an insight into the very heart of God

[1] Lambeth Report (1930), p. 69.

and realize that His nature and property is ever to have mercy and forgive, or, as another collect puts it, that it is "by showing mercy and pity," that He most truly "declares His almighty power," and His essential character.

NOTE

While writing this book I happened to come upon the following story:

"I came to Cuttack in answer to a heart-rending appeal from Madhu Sudan Das, a highly-educated man, though belonging to the ancient and separate Uriya race, which understands no human tongue but its own, and whose script looks like a wire netting of circular loops. He called himself a Christian also, though his faith was founded rather upon Christ than upon Roman Catholic, Anglican, or Nonconformist doctrines. For it was founded simply upon Christ's one prayer, 'Father, forgive them, for they know not what they do.' 'The man who could utter that prayer while dying under torture was divine,' he often said to me. 'The moment I heard that prayer I recognized that truth, and I have never doubted it since.' " (Nevinson, *More Changes and Chances*, p. 25.)

IX

Prayer

IF the character of God is such as we have been trying to describe, it follows that the closer the touch we can keep with Him the happier our lives will be. Whatever God's nature might have been, our dealings with Him would have been the most important part of human life, but those dealings might have been those of a slave with his master or of a servant with a lord whose purposes he did not even try to comprehend. We have been allowed to call God our Father, and to believe that we can in some measure understand His purpose for us, and it is a purpose in which all that is best in our nature urges us to co-operate, so that for Christians the task of keeping in touch with Him must be a happy one. It will not be easy, for He is so far above us, but, as the Psalmist told us, though God "hath His dwelling so high" yet "He humbleth Himself to behold the things that are in heaven and earth"; again there is much in our nature which urges us to be content with the things which we see and feel and know, but we all have something in us which "feels after God, if haply it may find Him" and encourages us to believe that "He is not far from everyone of us."

The most obvious method of keeping in touch with God is that of prayer, which sounds so easy and is in fact so hard. Christ showed us how important it was to pray, both by his words and by his example, and it has always played a large part in the Christian life, but the common way of regarding it is very unlike his own. To most people prayer means simply petition, and it is regarded as a way of getting something out of God which He is rather chary of granting. A moment's thought shows how false and inadequate this view is. If God is really in any sense our Father, He must wish to give to His children all that is best for them: in fact our Lord, in so many words, told us that the readiness of earthly fathers to give "good things" to their children is a faint picture of the good will of God: so that it is, or should be, plain from the first that there is no question of persuading an unwilling God to grant a favour which He is reluctant to bestow.

Again it can hardly be necessary to inform Him of our needs: once more, we have a word of Christ's which bears directly on the subject

—"Your Heavenly Father knoweth what things you have need of before you ask Him" —and a moment's thought shows us how unlikely it is that our knowledge of our own needs will be greater and more accurate than His.

The first and natural conclusion would be that petition is useless and uncalled for, but if we go back to the relationship of father and child which we have been encouraged to use we shall see that this conclusion is wrong. An earthly father may be very ready to give his child something, but the giving of the gift must depend on the frame of mind of the child who is to receive it. If something is claimed as a right, where no right to it exists, or if there is no reason to suppose that it will be properly used, a sensible father will postpone his gift until the moral situation has changed: he may have his own methods for deciding the point, and it is very reasonable that God's method should be to judge our fitness to receive anything by the way in which we ask for it, or rather by the frame of mind in which we ask it. We are bound to recognize that He knows best, and to be ready to accept His decision: if we demand something, and insist on our right to have it, we are, by the very form of our petition, showing our unfitness to receive.

But it may be said that this only applies to temporal things, to successes and blessings of that kind: if we are asking for good qualities, such as courage or humility, surely the question does not arise? It does not arise in the same form, but it is still necessary to consider the spirit in which the petition is made. Too many people assume that God is bound to answer such a prayer, and complain bitterly because they do not at once experience the result. But this is to assume that good qualities can be put into us from outside without any effort on our part: that would be magic, and all that we know of human life reminds us that God does not deal with man in that sort of way. It would have been perfectly easy for Him to make mankind perfect at the start, just as it would be easy for Him to turn a sinner into a saint in a moment, but He did not do it then and He does not do it now, because to do so would be to destroy human freedom and to make us mechanically good—and the goodness of a machine can have no moral value. What He does do is to hear our petition for a particular quality and to give us the opportunity, by His help, to win it, but we too often fail to see the opportunity and reject the help. A man who knows himself to be in danger of conceit may quite honestly pray for humility, but if he thereafter received a severe shock to his pride in himself he would be very likely to resent it and to fail to see that his prayer had been answered in the only effective way, or rather the only way consistent with giving him a share in working out his own deliverance from the danger.

When we pray for other people, which we do not do nearly enough, our prayers are free from the danger of selfishness and we can be sure that they are heard. Of course they are still liable to mistakes of ignorance, because we cannot be sure that the things we ask will be the best, but at any rate we shall be asking for what we believe to be good. It is perfectly true that we do not know *how* our prayers can be answered, and easy to say that one person's prayers cannot affect the life and character of another, but those who say this assume that our lives are in watertight compartments—a view which gets more and more incredible every day: we know that good words and good thoughts and kind actions (or the failure to speak and think and do them) have incalculable effects on the lives of other people, and it is a very curious assumption that in a God-governed world our prayers to Him can have no effect on other lives. In any case we are putting our prayers, so to speak, in His hands for Him to use if He

thinks fit, and (though it is a minor con-
sideration) there is nothing which so helps
us to behave rightly to other people as to
find a place for them in our prayers. It
seems strange at first sight that Christ encouraged us to pray for our enemies: it is
not so strange when we remember that the
real danger about our enemies is not that
they will behave badly to us but that we shall
behave badly to them, and from this danger
there is no remedy so secure as that of praying
for them. To pray for someone is to realize
his position as a son of God and a member
of God's family, and when we remember that,
enmity begins to disappear. Our enemy may
have many faults, but it is not a brother's
business to complain of his brother's failings.

But the fundamental mistake which we make
is, as has already been hinted, that we think
of prayer as primarily petition. It is doubtful
where the mistake begins, and probably it is
very deep-seated in human nature, but it has
certainly been helped by the Latin word for
to pray, which means nothing else than to beg.
The Romans were very practical people and
not great thinkers, so that it was natural for
them to concentrate on the practical and
almost tangible side of prayer, but it is an
error which has done a great deal of harm to
religion. If we look at the Lord's Prayer we

99

shall see at once how little petition it contains
in the ordinary sense of the word: the first
things we ask for are that God's purposes
should be fulfilled and His name, or nature,
honoured, and though these are technically
petitions there is clearly nothing selfish about
them. Once more, the prayer begins with
words which are a prayer in themselves, though
not a petition: there is an old story of a saint
and the consolation he gave to a boy who said
he had forgotten all the prayers he had been
taught: the saint encouraged him to keep on
saying Pater noster—our Father—the only two
words he could remember: to repeat those
words and meditate on their meaning is prayer
of the best and highest kind.

It is impossible to doubt that Christ's prayers
were mainly of this kind. It is not for us
to say how completely at any given moment
he realized what the will of the Father was,
but it is quite clear that his purpose throughout
his life was to realize it absolutely and to fulfil
it completely. We know that in the garden
of Gethsemane he felt a conflict between his
own natural will and that of God, but he
was able to pray that the latter should prevail:
though at first he asks that the cup may pass
from him we find him saying soon afterwards
"the cup which my Father hath given me,
shall I not drink it?" or, in other words, he

had made God's will his own, and that is, or should be, the character of all our prayers. If we once realize that God is absolutely good, and can will nothing but what is best, we shall not find it hard to surrender our own natural desires.

It is worth while to emphasize this point because we have got into the habit of saying "Thy will be done," as if it meant submitting to some decision which we cannot fully accept. That may indeed be so, as it was at first in Gethsemane, but only on comparatively rare occasions: the will of God for all men is that they should be as good, and, we may add, as happy, as is possible for them: we are so made that we are really happiest when fulfilling the purpose of our lives: the happiness which comes from "being good" is not as simple as the happiness of animals, for our nature is not as simple as theirs, but it is fundamentally of the same kind. What we ask at the beginning of the Lord's Prayer is that we and all men may come to understand God's true nature, and that we may live as people who do understand it, so that His will may be done throughout the world as it is done in Heaven by those who see Him face to face.

When we have said that, we have really said everything that needs to be said: we are in touch with Him, and "His will" covers

everything that is best for us and for all for
whom we desire to pray. We have only
further to ask that we and others may come
to understand it better and better, so that by
fulfilling it we may make the world the good
and happy place which He would have it be.
"He who rises from his knees a better man,
his prayer is answered."

X

Christian Practice

IN our attempts to find out what is the will of God for us and for other people our chief guide is, of course, the life and words of Jesus Christ. When we look at the Gospels from this point of view the first thing that strikes us is the absence of definite rules of life such, for instance, as those which Mahomet laid down for his followers. At first we are inclined to be disappointed, and some people like to point to the exactness with which Mahomet's orders are obeyed and contrast them with the feeble and distracted attempts of Christians to carry out their Master's instructions. This is so common a mistake that it is worth while to try to explain its origin.

Mahomet prided himself on his knowledge of human nature: he knew that the way to get things done is to make quite clear what you want and not to ask anything which is too difficult. He acted on these principles, and laid down exactly what prayers his followers were to say and how often they were to say them: how often they were to fast and what form their fasting was to take: how much they were to give in alms and so on. All these rules are excellent as far as they go, and they are also very easy to follow, for they save men the trouble of thinking for themselves, and that is a trouble which we are all very anxious to escape. But there are two great objections to them: in the first place, it is very bad for people not to be asked to think and tends to make all that they do mechanical and so valueless: and in the second, if you lay down rules, everyone will very naturally think that if you keep them you are perfect, and so all motive for improvement is taken away.

The result in Mahommedan countries has been just what might have been expected: the rules are very largely kept, but no progress is made, and that is why all rigidly Mahommedan countries have become the most backward in the world. Mahomet was a very great man, and many centuries in advance of his contemporaries, but he lived thirteen hundred years ago, and even if you allow that he was five hundred years ahead of the rest of the world, that leaves a long leeway to be made up, and a leeway which is always increasing, for as Mahomet definitely said that his revelation was final no orthodox Mahommedan has any motive for new discoveries and is actually breaking the prophet's rules if he tries to make any: so what was once, in many ways, a great progressive force has in time become one of the greatest hindrances to progress.

Christ's method was entirely different. "He knew what was in man," and was always finding that human nature was very feeble: even his disciples forsook him and fled, and we know how often they failed to understand him. But in spite of that he had a great belief in man, because he looked on all men as children of God who could be brought to understand Him. So, instead of laying down definite rules, which would have had to be adapted to the times in which he lived, he gave them great principles which they could apply, as they came to understand them, to all circumstances of life, and which could never get out of date. We have already seen two instances, those of slavery and the position of woman, in which Christians slowly learnt to apply his principles to their own lives, and that is what is always going on in Christian countries.

You can hardly think of a greater contrast than that between Mahomet laying down exact regulations and Jesus telling his very feeble followers to be "perfect." To a superficial observer the former seems so much the more sensible method, but the latter has the inestimable advantage that you can never suppose you have fulfilled it, and therefore must always be making new efforts. No doubt it is not so comfortable and easy-going a religion as the other, and no doubt many Christians take advantage of the absence of definite rules to keep no rules at all, but no one can doubt which takes the higher view of human nature, and pays it, so to speak, the greater compliment. It is quite true that no one can ever hope perfectly to fulfil Christ's command, but it is quite clear both from his words and from what we know of God's nature, that He values the effort more than the result. It is a very true saying that for the Christian there is no failure except in ceasing to try, and to go on trying is within the power of us all.

We see the same contrast when we compare Christ's teaching with that of John the Baptist. John was the last and greatest of the old prophets, but his religion, as we can see, was one purely of duty: he told men to be just, to abstain from violence, to be content with their wages, to repent of their sins. This is excellent advice, but it is not very inspiring. Christ, on the other hand, tells his followers never to be content with merely doing their duty. A Roman soldier, for instance, may have the power to compel a Jew to carry his baggage for one mile: the Christian Jew is to be ready to carry it for two: the first mile he does under a sense of compulsion, the second of his own free will, to save someone else from a tiresome piece of work. This is the *sweet doctrine of the second mile* and has a very clear inspiration in it: if he acts in this spirit, he that is least in the kingdom of heaven is greater than John the Baptist.

If we look, then, for the great principles which Jesus laid down, the first which strikes us is his demand for unselfishness. We ought to try to take the word in its literal sense and not merely to think of it in terms of those small acts which we call "self-denial." Jesus meant something very much greater than that. It is obvious that all of us are continually interested in ourselves, in what pleases us or pains us, and that we all tend to look at everything and everybody from a selfish point of view. Our own wants are the things which appeal to us most. This is the self which Christ told us to deny. He says that to seek self-satisfaction is to travel the wrong road and that he who seeks to save his life will lose it. This is a very profound saying, and means that our real "self" is something much deeper and nobler than we suppose. Just as we saw that life does not merely mean "keeping alive," so the "finding" or "saving of our self" means a great deal more than satisfying every selfish impulse that occurs to us.

Christ's remedy is that we should think of God and of our neighbour instead of thinking of ourselves: then we shall be "converted" in the literal sense of the word, for our heads will be turned round and we shall be facing in the right direction. So he took two great sayings from the Old Testament and adopted them as the two great commandments for his followers. It is foolish to think of them as if they were in any way opposed to one another, for it is only when we love God, which is the same thing as seeing Him as He is, that we shall properly understand why He made our neighbour and what He wants us to do for Him. No doubt many people who have a wrong idea of God, or no idea at all, show great practical love to their neighbours, but, as we have often said before, the better their theory the better their practice will be, and no Christian need be afraid that devotion to the first commandment will hamper him in fulfilling the second. Both commandments aim at taking us out of ourselves, which is the first thing that most of us need: it is a much greater danger that we shall think of ourselves too much than that we shall think too much of ourselves, for it is just as selfish to dwell overmuch on our own weaknesses as on our own virtues.

But Jesus was not content with merely laying down this principle: he proceeded to show in some detail how the principle affected the old commandments and in what spirit it should be carried into effect. And we should notice once more in passing what a tremendous claim this implied. The old law was given by God: it was He who, as every Jew believed, had spoken "to them of old time": and here was Christ, born a Jew and living among Jews, giving legislation of his own as of equal authority: "ye have heard that it was said to them of old time" . . . "but I say unto you." It was impossible for those who heard him to doubt that he was claiming divine authority.

When we come to the particular commandments with which he dealt we see that he treated them all in the same way. First of all he made them all a matter not of doing or not doing particular acts, but of living in a particular spirit. An earthly judge has to go in the main by what is actually done: a murderer or a thief to him is a man who has done, or at least attempted to do, a particular crime: but God, who can read the hearts of men, judges them by their desires, whether they take effect or not, and this is clearly just. A man who plans a burglary or a murder and does not commit it because of the inconvenient presence of the police is no *better* a man than he would have been if the police had not happened to be there. And Christ goes right down to the very heart of the matter.   Murder springs from hatred and a Christian must not hate: theft springs from the desire wrongfully to obtain what belongs to someone else, and that desire a Christian must not feel: adultery, which is a wrongful act, springs from those wrong thoughts and wrong passions which a Christian must control.

Again he is not satisfied with teaching us to restrain and control the desires which are wrong: he wishes to fill us with the positive desire to do what is right.   The simplest example is in the case of the eighth commandment.   To steal, as we have said, implies a desire to get by any means what is our neighbour's and to keep it for ourself: the Christian commandment is to be generous, which means giving to our neighbours what is legitimately our own.[1]   St. Paul's advice to the converted thief sums up the whole matter very clearly: "let him that stole steal no more, but rather let him labour, working with his hands the thing that is good, that he may have to give to him that needeth": it is impossible to imagine a more complete "conversion": the world, for that particular criminal, is indeed "turned upside-down."

[1] It is often forgotten that the man in the parable who said "Is it not lawful for me to do what I will with mine own?" said it to justify himself for being unreasonably generous.

But the most fundamental and characteristic of all the positive Christian commands is to love, and just because it is so important and so insistent it has been the most misunderstood. Everyone knows how charity, which originally meant nothing but love in the purest sense, has been degraded to mean the mere giving away of money, without any regard to what it costs the giver, and many people who do not fall into that mistake think of it as meaning nothing but a kind of vague amiability, or a mere negative unwillingness to do harm. Christian love is something very different from that: it has nothing to do with "liking people", which is a mere emotion and may have no merit in it: it means trying to do what is best for other people, no matter how "unattractive" they may be, or however great may be the cost. It is clear that this involves trying to understand them, and to realize that they matter as much to themselves, and to God, as we do to ourselves, and this is a very hard thing to achieve. Our sympathy must be as like as possible to that of Christ himself, who saw the good in every man and helped it to come to light.

What we think of other people is often of more value than anything that we actually do to or for them; we know how much we are affected by the opinion which other people hold of us, and it is not too much to say that most of what is good in us is due to those who think us better than we are: here is a tremendous power which we have of helping other people, by deliberately choosing to look on their best side: it is the most important part of the Golden Rule that we should do to others as we would have them do to us. We often forget that that is laid down in the Catechism as being our "duty" and indeed it is the central part of a Christian's obligation so far as his neighbours are concerned. God, we are told, declares His almighty power most chiefly in showing mercy and pity: we all have the chance of showing power in that divine way, but very seldom use it.

It does not need to be emphasized how quickly our own society, and indeed the world at large, would be changed if Christian principles prevailed, or even if Christian people always carried them into practice: they *have* prevailed, as we have seen, to some extent, but there are many more fields into which they should be carried, and it is a process which can be begun at once and on the smallest scale. If you wish to understand what it would mean you cannot do better than read St. Paul's words to the Ephesians, and remember, as you read, that they are addressed to people who had no Christian background, but had themselves very recently been leading heathen lives in a typical heathen city. "Putting away lying, speak every man truth with his neighbour, for we are members one of another: be ye angry and sin not: let not the sun go down on your wrath, neither give place to the devil. Let him that stole steal no more but rather let him labour working with his hands the thing that is good that he may have to give to him that needeth. Let no corrupt communication proceed out of your mouth but such as is good for edifying as the need may be, that it may minister grace unto the hearers ... Let all bitterness, and wrath, and anger, and clamour, and evil speaking, be put away from you with all malice, and be ye kind one to another, tender-hearted, forgiving one another, even as God for Christ's sake hath forgiven you."

NOTE

It may seem strange that nothing has been said of Christ's attitude towards riches: the simple fact is that he thought very much less of the question than we do. It is quite clear that he definitely considered riches as a handicap: this is so far from our own view that we fail to appreciate it: it is doubtful whether there was any grinding poverty in his time: certainly when he said that "the poor" were blessed he was thinking not of the destitute, but of those who were not entangled with the cares of this world, as the rich tend to be. He did not tell all men to "sell all that they had," though he did prescribe that remedy for one particular young man; but he repeatedly warned his hearers of the danger of caring too much for their earthly possessions. The celebrated sentence about the dangers of riches is most naturally translated, "it is easier for a camel to go through the eye of a needle than for a man to enter rich into the kingdom of God," and, if it is thought that we have turned a paradox into a platitude, it must be allowed that it is a platitude which we are all very ready to forget.

XI

The Sacraments

THE Christian sacraments are, as the Prayer Book tells us, "outward and visible signs" of the great realities of our relationship with God. It is easy to see the value of such outward signs, because, human nature being what it is, they convey a meaning more clearly than mere words can. When, after one of St. Paul's sermons, those who wished to join the Christian fellowship were invited to be baptized we can realize how the ceremony must have impressed its meaning on those who witnessed it. The convert was washed in the water, and everyone understands the purpose of washing: the water closed over his head and his old life with all its failures had disappeared: he rose from the water a new man, and the white garments in which he was clothed showed both that he was cleansed from the past and that he was hopeful for the future. By our custom of infant baptism we have lost some of the symbolism, but its main purpose remains clear:

a simple act of which everyone understands
the meaning has become the outward and
visible sign of the Grace of God which cleanses
us from past sin and gives us that fresh start
which we need.[1]

Even so we do not fully understand its
meaning unless we remember that the heathen
world believed that sin could never be wiped
out or cleansed away: after all, that is not an
"unnatural" belief, for nature does not forgive:
if you put your hand in the fire, however sorry
you may afterwards be, the injury and the scar
remain. And so, as those who have read
Greek tragedies will remember, the Greeks
believed that when sin once got into a house
the innocent descendants had to pay for the
guilt of their ancestor: the Jews went through
a similar stage, as one of their commandments

[1] The practice of infant baptism arose for practical reasons.
When Christian parents were living in the midst of a heathen
society they naturally wished their children to be marked out
from the first as belonging to God, or "within the covenant,"
and saved from the risk of having to join in heathen practices
which were often very undesirable. They did not suppose
that by baptizing their children they could "make them
Christians," for being a Christian means accepting the faith
with one's reason and one's will, but they wished to put
them on the right road (as a modern parent may put the
name of his infant son down for a club or a school) and they
had a good answer ready to those who criticized their bring-
ing little children to Christ: the disciples had been rebuked
for making just the same criticism.

shows, and, though the prophets had denied that children suffered for their fathers' sin, the belief died hard. To the ancient world as a whole the doctrine that sins could be forgiven was the most appealing part of the gospel—"the good news" which they most desired to hear, so that a baptism meant more to them than we can easily imagine.

When we come to the other great Christian sacrament we see that the same fundamental principle is employed: Christ takes the simplest of ideas and gives it a spiritual meaning: just as everyone understands the significance of washing, so everyone understands why we eat and drink. We do so to keep our bodies alive; without nourishment they would starve and die. No one feels any difficulty in extending the idea to the brain: if a man's brain is not given nourishment by fresh ideas it will be starved. What Christ does is to extend the metaphor to the soul or spirit, which is, as we have already seen, that part of us which matters most, the part in which our real life may be said to lie. And what is the food of the soul? No Christian can doubt of the answer: it is Christ's life, Christ's spirit, Christ's example, or in one word Christ himself. Every time that we come to the Communion we come hoping to receive into ourselves some of that divine power by which he lived and spoke. We shall not receive it all, because of our inability to receive and to retain, but we shall receive according to the measure of our faith and to the honesty of our seeking.

If this language seems extravagant we shall remember that a good action, if it is really good, is, as far as it goes, perfect: a small act of real self-sacrifice is, we may reverently say, perfect. We all of us have risen to perfection for some tiny portions of our lives: what we ask in the Holy Communion is for more of that perfect spirit. The paramount miracle is that we should ever want to aim at perfection and ever, even for a moment, succeed: there is no additional miracle in our receiving strength from coming into contact with the Source of all Strength through our faith in Christ who made his nature clear.

This is one simple way of approaching the subject, but there is another which to some people seems simpler still. It is certain that Christ on the last evening of his earthly life sat with his disciples at a common meal: that he then performed certain actions and said certain words, and that he commanded his disciples to do what he had then done "in remembrance" of him. From this point of view our service is a fulfilment of that command, and to "remember" Christ is the supreme duty of Christians. But we are not merely remembering Christ: we are remembering him as he was on a special occasion, and the more we realize what that occasion was the fuller and deeper our remembrance will become. He had just dismissed Judas, knowing quite well what he was going to do: he knew that he had only a very few more hours to live on earth before his blood would be shed and his body broken on the Cross. *At that moment* he institutes this memorial service: the bread is broken bread: the wine is a token of blood that is shed: what they are bidden to remember is the supreme self-sacrifice of their Master, and to remember it must mean, in however feeble a degree, to try to copy it in their lives.

It would seem that both roads lead to a very similar conclusion, for if to "remember" Christ must mean to wish to follow him, and if we can only follow him by receiving some of his spirit into ourselves, those who speak of the Lord's Supper and those who speak of Communion, or fellowship with him, mean the same thing. It is a very distressing fact that Christians have been, and are, so much divided as to the method by which God bestows the gift which all alike hope to receive. Controversies about the "Real presence" would lose much of their bitterness if all remembered, what no Christian can doubt, that God is really present everywhere—that His presence, in fact, is the one supreme reality—and that no moral gift can be given by any ceremony, however holy, except to those whose hearts and minds are fit to receive it. It is an inexorable law of the spiritual life that we receive *in proportion* to what we give, though mercifully we are always receiving from God far more than either we consciously desire or morally deserve.

A great deal of the trouble comes from the instinctive belief of many people that what can be seen and handled has a special reality of its own. In fact the things which we believe to be most real are not of this kind. Loyalty and honour are more real than the things for which men fight and pain is more real, in the true sense of the word, than the broken leg which causes it, because a leg, though a perfectly real thing, is not *so* real as the person to whom it belongs. To a Christian Love is the supreme reality, and though whatever symbolizes or conveys it is worthy of high honour, we must never confuse the symbol or sign with what it signifies.[1] The compilers of our Prayer Book condemned the idea that Christ was present in the sacrament in corporal or bodily form, but they were careful not to deny his real presence, which

[1] See Note at end of chapter.

is indeed promised by his own words to any two or three who are gathered together in his name. It is quite legitimate to affirm his presence in a special sense in the Sacrament which he so solemnly instituted, but this must not be taken as a denial of his presence elsewhere.

Another word which has given rise to infinite disputes is the word Sacrifice. With primitive peoples sacrifice was instituted as a means of appeasing or propitiating God either (in the earliest times of all) by supplying his needs, or by the willing surrender of some valued possession. The Jews passed through this stage, and their great Psalmists and prophets made it clear to them that the only real sacrifice was self-sacrifice. "In whole burnt offerings and sacrifices for sin thou hadst no pleasure: then said I, Lo I am come to do thy will, O God. He taketh away the first that he may establish the second." This teaching prevailed, and in the Book of Leviticus we find the whole emphasis laid on the way in which the worshipper identifies himself with the offering which he makes: its blood, or life, represents the offering of himself. That idea is preserved in our Communion service when we say that "we offer ourselves, our souls and bodies to be a reasonable holy and lively (or living) sacrifice": unfortunately many of our hymns and some of our books of devotion use the words in their old sense and this leads to much confusion, especially among people unaccustomed to the idea. If we remember that blood in this connection means the sacrificed life we should escape many false ideas. The Sacrifice which Christ offered is that of his life willingly surrendered, and it was a perfect and final sacrifice because of the perfection of that life. It is in the spirit of that sacrifice that we make our own small sacrifices—very small in themselves, but ennobled by the spirit in which they are made, and it is, as we believe, the continual help and guidance of God, given in sacrament and answered prayer, which makes our offerings not unworthy to be accepted.

So we find that, from whatever angle we approach it and whatever words we use, the great Christian Sacrament sums up and enforces the great Christian lesson of unselfishness. We have to be ready to surrender our own prejudices and selfish desires that we may receive the Divine spirit: we have to follow the Divine example of self-surrender: we have to learn to sacrifice ourselves as Christ sacrificed himself. We may not be called upon to do so in dramatic fashion: but if we begin by sacrificing our laziness or our bad temper (which we should be glad to part with) or some of the comforts and pleasures which we could well spare, we shall have taken a first step along the road, and shall be encouraged to persevere. Opportunities for such self-denial are never far to seek, but are to be found in "the trivial round and common task," and it is very certain that, when found and accepted, they are, in very truth, "a road to bring us daily nearer God."

NOTE

The nature of a sign, or symbol, may be made clearer by two examples. A kiss is a sign of love: a pound note is a symbol for a certain amount of money. Neither has any value *in itself*: the one depends on the sentiments with which it is given, the other on the power to pay of those who issue it: and no one can doubt which is the higher kind of value. A sacrament has some of the characteristics of each kind of symbol. We have no doubt of the power behind it, but because it belongs to the higher type it depends also on the good faith of those who receive. A pound note keeps its value whatever may be the character of the man who gives or receives it, but the kiss of Judas showed not love but treachery, and those who receive a sacrament for unworthy reasons must blame themselves if they get no benefit from it. It is "the faithful" by whom the promised blessings are "verily and indeed taken and received."

XII

The Holy Spirit [1]

THE Christian life is described by St. Paul as a life "in the Spirit," and there can be no doubt as to what spirit he means: indeed he uses the phrase as an alternative to his other phrase "in Christ." The Christian is to hope and pray and believe that Christ's spirit will guide his every action.

As to the general nature of that spirit there can be no doubt: as we have already said, the spirit in which Christ lived his earthly life is one which is quite unmistakable, nor could any mistake have been made if we had always remembered that he speaks of the sending of the Holy Spirit as being in a real sense his own coming back to the world.[2] But this

[1] No attempt is made in this chapter (for reasons suggested on page 60) to deal with the metaphysical questions raised by the doctrine of the Trinity. For our present purpose it is enough to say that the God who "spake in time past unto the Fathers by the prophets," and to a later generation "in His Son," speaks to us still by the Spirit sent "in Christ's name."

[2] John xiv, 16 ff.

central truth has been too often forgotten and has led to misapprehensions which we must try to remove.

In the first place, through an accident of language, the name the Holy Ghost has suggested an indefiniteness, and even an unreality, which has disastrous results. The spirit of Christ is a perfectly definite thing which we know in theory and can recognize in practice. We are in no danger, if we think for a moment, of doubting that the "spirit" in which things are done is more important than the things themselves and indeed gives them their real meaning.[1]

Again, the word "Comforter" (especially when associated with the symbolism of the dove) is apt to give a misleading impression. The word means Strengthener, and the strength of Christ's character is shown not only in his power of "comforting" the sorrowful and the sick but in his power of denouncing and resisting evil. St. John the Baptist associated the Holy Spirit with "fire," and that symbolism is more appropriate to the title we are considering. The liturgical colour for Whit-Sunday is scarlet —that colour which the blind man described

[1] The insistence on the spirit in which things are done is one of the points which distinguishes Christianity from Mohammedanism. No public-school boy can fail to see the danger of living by an external code.

as the blast of a trumpet—and the Spirit of Christ is one which should enable his followers to fight under his banner and in his strength against the manifold evils of the world.

Nor should it be forgotten, as it so often is, that the gifts of the Holy Spirit are far from being merely "moral" in the narrow sense of the word. The inspiration for which we ask, for instance, in the *Veni Creator* is largely, if not mainly, intellectual, and the spirit of wisdom, understanding and counsel is inseparable from that of true godliness: we must never forget that we are bidden to serve God "with all our mind," and this is one of the duties which the Holy Spirit enables us to fulfil, guiding us "into all the truth."

Once more, there are those who regard the Holy Spirit as essentially a personal and individual possession: this is far from being the doctrine of the Christian Church. It is promised to Christ's followers as members of the Christian body: they are enrolled in it at baptism, they take up their full membership at Confirmation, and it is of members of that body that the New Testament speaks. There is no need to deny (nor does the New Testament deny) that the gift may be given to others, for *Deus non tenetur sacramentis suis* (God is not limited by His own ordinances), but there is no doubt that St. Paul had in mind a Christian

126

society actuated by a common spirit, and that spirit the spirit of Christ. Mr. Wesley was right when he said that "the Bible knows nothing of solitary religion."

If we turn from such mistaken views to the question what precisely the Christian spirit is, we shall not have to look far for our definition. The "fruit of the Spirit," says St. Paul, "is love, joy, peace, longsuffering, kindness, goodness, faithfulness, meekness, temperance." By these "fruits" Christ's disciples are to be known. It is by the grace of the same spirit that they are to think of the things which are true, honourable, just, pure, lovely and of good report, and to put away from themselves bitterness, wrath, anger and all malice. They are to live in Christ's own way.

It is because we, as Christians, have in ourselves "the first-fruits of the Spirit" that we "groan within ourselves" at the manifold imperfections of the world, but at the same time we believe ourselves to have the remedy for its troubles. By the Spirit within us we dimly realize God's purpose for the world and are able, if we will, to co-operate with it by our actions and our prayers. Every Christian who is endeavouring to live his life in Christ's spirit is making his contribution to the Divine purpose, and as he so endeavours will learn more of what that purpose is. He will see it in the small concerns of his own life, and will come to a clearer sense of the moral basis on which any Christian society must rest: he will welcome any signs that in national or international or ecclesiastical affairs the unmistakable Christian spirit is beginning to prevail: he will feel himself a free man, for "where the Spirit of the Lord is, there is liberty," but his freedom will be that which the Psalmist had in mind when he wrote "I will walk at liberty, for I seek Thy commandments."

"God makes Himself known not to His critics but to His disciples": He does not, as many have disastrously believed, make Himself known through an infallible Church or an infallible Bible which would save men the trouble of using their minds: to love Him, and to endeavour to do His will, is the way to know of the doctrine, and a Christian lives by his faith in his Master's promise, "If a man love me, he will keep my word: and my Father will love him, and we will come unto him and make our abode with him." Such a man will indeed enjoy that for which we so often pray—the grace of our Lord Jesus Christ, the love of God and the fellowship of the Holy Spirit.

Epilogue

WE have tried to give an outline of Christianity in the three aspects which we mentioned at the beginning. We have seen it first as a system of thought which claims to give an explanation of the world, as made by a good God, who reveals Himself in other ways but most clearly in man, made after His own image, with a divine spark in him which can be fanned into flame. To such a world it is natural that the supreme revelation should be given by an Incarnation, by God's showing Himself in and through a human life, and we have seen how Christ's life on earth shows forth both what God eternally is and what man might be.

Then we have seen, as a matter of history, the use which men have made of this divine revelation. The more we expect of the Christian Church, the more we shall no doubt be disappointed at its record in history, but it has done enough to prove its claim to have the remedy for the troubles of the world, and it has failed only because Christians have been afraid to employ it fearlessly. In our day Christianity no longer holds an unchallenged position: it is attacked both on the side of theory and on that of practice, and this constitutes a call to all Christians both to understand their religion better and to apply it more courageously. The increase of human knowledge can be nothing but a gain to those who believe that all Truth is one, so that all discoveries help us better to understand God, the Maker of all things visible and invisible. On the side of practice we are called upon to show the Christian virtues in action, for the critics (except those who merely want an excuse for living as they like) would cease to criticize if they saw that Christians really meant what they said. There are many grounds for hope, and not least is the astounding change which has come over missionary work in the last century and has made it clear that the character and teaching of Christ have a unique appeal to men of every race and colour. We have to face a vastly enlarged world, but we believe that we have the one answer to all its needs.

We have seen how national Churches came to arise and among them our Church of England, and how it strives to perform the double task of being loyal to ancient tradition and of welcoming new truth. This effort exposes it to attack from every side and to the sneers of those who call it a church of compromise clinging to the middle path. These attacks will not disturb those who believe that truth usually lies in the middle between two extremes, and that to be honest in the pursuit of truth is one of the highest of all human qualities. It may certainly be said that there is no Church which, by its firm hold on sound tradition and by its readiness to learn, is better fitted to be the rallying point of Christendom in the future.

Finally, we have sketched in outline some of the leading characteristics of the Christian life, and shown how that life is based on the revelation of God given by Jesus Christ, and supported by the continual gift of his Holy Spirit, in sacrament and in answered prayer. No outline can do more than the barest justice to the fulness of that revelation, or to the manysidedness of Christ's character. We have tried to show some of its more salient characteristics, sufficient to encourage those who wish to make a start. As they study Christ's life and teaching they will continually find new paths opening before them, for it remains true, as St. Paul wrote many centuries ago, that "in him are all the treasures of wisdom and knowledge hidden"— hidden, but only that they may become revealed to those who humbly and patiently seek to find.

Lord of Beauty, Thine the splendour
Shown in earth and sky and sea,
Burning sun and moonlight tender,
Hill and river, flower and tree:
Lest we fail our praise to render,
Touch our eyes that we may see!

Lord of Wisdom, Whom obeying
Mighty waters ebb and flow,
While unhasting, undelaying,
Planets on their courses go;
In Thy laws Thyself displaying,
Teach our minds Thy Truth to know!

Lord of Life, alone sustaining
All below and all above,
Lord of Love, by Whose ordaining
Sun and stars sublimely move:
In our earthly spirits reigning,
Lift our hearts that we may love!

Lord of Beauty, bid us own Thee,
Lord of Truth, our footsteps guide,
Till, as Love our hearts enthrone Thee,
And, with vision purified,
Lord of All when all have known Thee,
Thou in all art glorified!